# LAWYERING AND ETHICS FOR THE BUSINESS ATTORNEY

By

**Marc I. Steinberg**
*Radford Professor of Law*
*Southern Methodist University*



AMERICAN CASEBOOK SERIES®

THOMSON
WEST

Mat #18372444

610 Opperman Drive
P.O. Box 64526
St. Paul, MN 55164–0526
1–800–328–9352


Printed in the United States of America

**ISBN** 0–314–25838–8

*TEXT IS PRINTED ON 10% POST CONSUMER RECYCLED PAPER*

# Acknowledgments

I owe many thanks to my research assistants, colleagues, and lawyer-friends for their assistance. My research assistants deserve kudos for their outstanding work—Rob Castle, Barrett Howell, Brooks Leavitt, Dustin Mauck, Bobby Moore, Bipasha Mukherjee, and Jason Myers. In particular, Mr. Howell and Mr. Myers, both now practicing with prestigious law firms, successfully undertook several challenging assignments with respect to this project.

I thank my friends and colleagues at SMU for their support on this project: Dean John Attanasio, Professors Bill Bridge, Alan Bromberg, Linda Eads, Shubha Ghosh, Chris Hanna, George Martinez, and Fred Moss, as well as Ms. Jan Spann and Ms. Carolyn Yates. My thanks to the SMU Dedman School of Law for the award of summer research grants in connection with this project. Also, I thank the SMU Maguire Center for Ethics and Public Responsibility for support of this project, and in particular, Mr. Cary Maguire, Professor Richard Mason, and Ms. Lorren Timberman. Moreover, my thanks to my lawyer-friends for their input on this project: Orrin Harrison, Ralph Janvey, Frank Razzano, Darrel Rice, and Bob Wise.

Permission has been granted from the American Bar Association, the American Law Institute, and the Missouri Law Review to use certain excerpts herein. In particular: (1) The ABA Model Rules of Professional Conduct, the ABA Model Code of Professional Responsibility, and ABA Formal Opinions 92–366, 98–410, and 00–418. Reprinted by permission of the American Bar Association (the foregoing ABA documents are available from Service Center, American Bar Association, 750 North Lake Shore Drive, Chicago, IL 60611–4497, 1–800–285–2221); (2) American Law Institute, Restatement of the Law, The Law Governing Lawyers. Reprinted by permission of the American Law Institute; and (3) Aibel, Corporate Counsel and Business Ethics: A Personal Review reprinted by permission of the Missouri Law Review, Copyright 1994 by the Curators of the University of Missouri.

I dedicate this book with all my love to my beautiful wife Laurie and my wonderful children Alexandra (Alex), Avram (Avi) and Phillip (Bear).

*

# Summary of Contents



*

# Table of Contents



*

# LAWYERING AND ETHICS FOR THE BUSINESS ATTORNEY

*

# Scenario I

## WHO'S THE CLIENT?

When an individual visits a lawyer's office and asks to be represented in a particular matter, the attorney normally has little difficulty identifying who is the client. Entity representation, however, renders the attorney's client-identification process more complex. The importance of ascertaining the identity of the client is underscored by the American Bar Association's (ABA) Model Rules of Professional Conduct. These Rules impose certain obligations that run from the attorney to the client.[1] For example, Model Rule 1.7 focuses on the loyalty owed by the attorney to each client.[2] Similarly, Model Rule 1.6 requires the attorney to maintain confidentiality with respect to information relating to the representation of a client.[3] This confidentiality is premised on two separate, but related, legal doctrines.[4]

The principle of confidentiality under the Model Rules is based first on the attorney-client privilege, which generally protects written or oral communications that relate to the providing of legal advice to the client.[5]

**1.** *See, e.g.,* ABA Model Rules of Prof. Conduct, Rules 1.3–1.8.

**2.** As comment one to the rule states: "Loyalty and independent judgment are essential elements in the lawyer's relationship to a client."

**3.** *See* Rule 1.6 of the Model Rules.

**4.** *Id.* cmt. 5.

**5.** As used in the Model Rules, the work product doctrine is included in the attorney-client privilege. *Id. See Upjohn*

The second principle premised on lawyer-client confidentiality is found in the Model Rules themselves.[6] Lawyer-client confidentiality is more encompassing than the attorney-client privilege: Regardless whether the information is protected from disclosure under the attorney-client privilege, Rule 1.6 mandates (with certain exceptions) that all information relating to the representation of that client, regardless of its source, be kept confidential.[7] Both the privilege and the attorney's confidentiality obligation contain certain exceptions. For example, when the client gives informed consent to the disclosure of the otherwise protected information, such information is no longer within the scope of Rule 1.6.[8] Moreover, certain information is deemed to be "impliedly authorized" by the client in the course of carrying out the representation.[9] A lawyer under the Model Rules also may reveal client information to the extent necessary "to prevent the client from committing a criminal act that the lawyer believes is likely to result in imminent death or substantial bodily harm."[10]

Model Rule 1.6's obligations encompass communications between an attorney and a client.[11] An entity, such as a corporation, clearly cannot speak for itself; rather it must rely on and speak through its representatives. Under the Model Rules, these corporate representatives are defined as constituents.[12] Constituents include directors, officers, employees, members, and sharehold-

*Co. v. United States*, 449 U.S. 383 (1981).

**6.** *See* Rule 1.6 of the Model Rules.

**7.** *Id.* Rule 1.6 cmt. 5.

**8.** *See* Revised Rule 1.6(a).

**9.** Unless the client instructs otherwise, the attorney is impliedly authorized to disclose certain information. For example, lawyers within the same firm are generally deemed to have implied authorization to share client information with each other, to the extent necessary to carry out the representation. *See* Rule 1.6 cmts. 7–8.

**10.** Model Rule 1.6(b)(1). A lawyer also may reveal client information to the extent necessary to establish a claim or defense on behalf of the lawyer in the event a controversy arises between the client and the lawyer. Model Rule 1.6(b)(2).

**11.** *Id.* Model Rule 1.6(a).

**12.** *Id.* Model Rule 1.13.

ers.[13] The communications between the attorney and a constituent of the organization relating to the giving of legal advice are within the scope of Rule 1.6, so long as the communications relate to the constituent's role or position within the organization.[14] In a situation where the organization's attorney becomes aware of a constituent's contemplated course of action that is a violation of law that reasonably may be imputed to the organization, the Model Rules provide a series of procedures that the attorney should follow, depending on the severity of the potential harm.[15] In the most extreme situation, the attorney may find it necessary to refer the matter to the organization's highest authority.[16] This issue is addressed in later Scenarios of this text. In the event that the organization's highest authority insists upon conduct that violates the law and that likely will result in substantial harm to the organization, the attorney may withdraw from the representation, in accordance with Model Rule 1.16.[17]

Closely held corporations (such as family corporations) may present complex scenarios. The attorney for such an enterprise often has significant contact with many, if not all, of the constituents.[18] As a result, some of the constituents may think that the attorney is representing them as individuals, in addition to the business enterprise.[19] Indeed, some sources argue that due to the close nature of these corporations, the attorney's actions have a direct effect on each constituent and consequently, the attorney's obligations should run not only to the

**13.** *Id.* Model Rule 1.13(d).

**14.** *Id.* Model Rule 1.13 cmt. 2.

**15.** *Id.* Model Rule 1.13(b) & cmt. 3.

**16.** *Id.* Model Rule 1.13(b)(3) & cmt. 4.

**17.** *Id.* Model Rules 1.13(c), 1.16(a)–(b). *See* C. Wolfram, *Modern Legal Ethics* § 13.7 (1986).

**18.** *See* Mitchell, *Professional Responsibility and the Close Corporation: Toward a Realistic Ethic*, 74 Cornell L. Rev. 466 (1989).

**19.** *See* Haynsworth, *Competent Counseling of Small Business Clients*, 13 U.C. Davis L. Rev. 401 (1980); Mitchell, note 18 *supra*.

organization, but to each constituent as well.[20] In a family corporation, for example, the constituents are generally the employees, shareholders, officers and directors of the enterprise.[21] In addition, the business operations of a closely held corporation are oftentimes the sole source of livelihood for its shareholders. In such a situation, the corporation's success takes on paramount importance to each shareholder; if things go sour, such shareholders have no viable escape from their investment.[22] These problems are exacerbated when individual shareholders have different personal interests, and each attempts to implement his/her individual goal within the company's policies and corporate framework.

It should be noted that in the partnership context, some courts have found that the attorney representing the organization also represents the individual partners.[23] As one court explained: "In the context of the representation of a partnership, the attorney for the partnership represents all the partners as to matters of partnership business."[24] Under this approach, an individual partner (even under privity principles) may bring a malpractice suit against the organization's attorney. Such was the situation in *Adell* where the court allowed a limited partner to file a malpractice claim against the attorney that had been retained on behalf of the limited partnership.[25] Other courts, however, have adhered to the entity theory of representation in the partnership

**20.** Mitchell, *supra* note 18, 74 Cornell L. Rev. at 506. *See In re Brownstein*, 602 P.2d 655 (Or.1979). *But see Skarbrevik v. Cohen, England & Whitfield*, 282 Cal.Rptr. 627 (Ct.App.1991).

**21.** *See, e.g., Galler v. Galler*, 203 N.E.2d 577 (Ill.1964); *Triggs v. Triggs*, 385 N.E.2d 1254 (N.Y.1978).

**22.** *See* Hendon, *Combatting Legal Theft: Arguments For Shareholder/Employees Terminated From Close Corporations*, 77 Or. L. Rev. 735, 737 (1998).

**23.** *See e.g. Adell v. Sommers, Schwartz, Silver and Schwartz*, 428 N.W.2d 26 (Mich. Ct.App.1988).

**24.** *Wortham & Van Liew v. Superior Court*, 233 Cal.Rptr. 725, 728 (Ct.App.1987).

**25.** *Adell v. Sommers, Schwartz, Silver and Schwartz*, 428 N.W.2d 26, 30 (Mich.Ct. App.1988).

setting.[26] Consequently, depending on the jurisdiction and the underlying circumstances, it may be uncertain whether an attorney for a partnership represents only the enterprise, or, absent an agreement otherwise, is deemed to represent the individuals as well.

An attorney for a newly forming or formed corporation should discuss potentially significant issues and conflicts before they arise. When representing a closely held corporation, the attorney should monitor the situations in which significant adverse interests may arise. The need for caution results from the fact that in close corporations the interests and rights of the organization and the constituents who control the organization often start off as consistent with one another.[27] Perhaps because of this alignment of interests, at least some courts take the position that, unless the parties agree otherwise, the attorney represents the constituents in their individual capacities as well as the organization.[28] This approach, however, is contrary to the generally accepted "entity" rule, according to which the entity (or the organization) is the client, and not the individual shareholders.[29]

Under the entity rule, "where a lawyer represents a corporation, the client is the corporation, not the corporation's shareholders."[30] As explained by one court:

> "[W]here an attorney represents a closely held corporation, the attorney [normally] . . . owes no separate duty of diligence and care to an individual shareholder. . . . [A]n attorney representing a corporation does not become the attorney for the individid-

**26.** *See, e.g., Hopper v. Frank,* 16 F.3d 92 (5th Cir.1994) (applying Mississippi law).

**27.** *See, e.g., Wilkes v. Springside Nursing Home, Inc.*, 353 N.E.2d 657 (Mass.1976).

**28.** *See e.g. In re Brownstein*, 602 P.2d 655 (Or.1979), *citing, In re Banks*, 584 P.2d 284 (Or.1978).

**29.** *See, e.g. Skarbrevik v. Cohen, England & Whitfield*, 282 Cal.Rptr. 627 (Ct.App.1991); *Egan v. McNamara*, 467 A.2d 733 (D.C.App.1983); *Jesse v. Danforth*, 485 N.W.2d 63 (Wis. 1992).

**30.** *McKinney v. McMeans*, 147 F.Supp.2d 898, 901 (M.D.Tenn.2001).

ual stockholders merely because the attorney's actions on behalf of the corporation may also benefit the stockholders. The duty of an attorney for a corporation is first and foremost to the corporation, even though the legal advice rendered to the corporation may affect the shareholders.'' [31]

Contrary to the ''entity'' theory of representation,[32] some courts take the position that counsel represents individual shareholders in addition to the organization, based on each such shareholder's reasonable expectation of being separately represented.[33] As one court explained: ''Although, in the ordinary corporate situation, corporate counsel does not necessarily become counsel for the corporation's shareholders ... where, as here, the corporation is a close corporation consisting of only two shareholders with equal interests in the corporation, it is indeed reasonable for each shareholder to believe that the corporate counsel is in effect his own individual attorney.''[34] To hold otherwise, reasoned the court, would ''exalt form over substance.''[35]

Ascertaining whether such a reasonable expectation exists may hinge on the frequency and quality of encounters between the attorney and the individual. Elements that have been deemed relevant in this determination include: ''[T]he extent and nature of the attor-

**31.** *Brennan v. Ruffner*, 640 So.2d 143, 145–146 (Fla.Dist.Ct. App.1994). *See SEC. v. Credit Bancorp, Ltd.*, 96 F.Supp.2d 357 (S.D.N.Y.2000).

**32.** *See* cases cited *supra* notes 29–31.

**33.** *See e.g.*, Comment, *An Expectations Approach to Client Identity*, 106 Harv. L. Rev. 687 (1993).

**34.** *Rosman v. Shapiro*, 653 F.Supp. 1441, 1445 (S.D.N.Y. 1987), *citing*, *Westinghouse Electric Corp. v. Kerr–McGee Corp.*, 580 F.2d 1311 (7th Cir. 1978), *Glover v. Libman*, 578 F.Supp. 748 (N.D.Ga.1983), *Bobbitt v. Victorian House, Inc.*, 545 F.Supp. 1124 (N.D.Ill.1982). *See generally* S. Gillers, *Regulation of Lawyers* 566–571 (6th ed. 2002); G. Hazard, S. Koniak & R. Cramton, *The Law and Ethics of Lawyering* 759–768 (3d ed. 1999); T. Morgan & R. Rotunda, *Professional Responsibility–Problems and Materials* 293–295 (7th ed. 2000); J. Sutton & J. Dzienkowski, *Professional Responsibility of Lawyers* 108–111 (2d ed. 2002).

**35.** 653 F.Supp. at 1445.

ney's representation of the constituent in individual matters, the attorney's representation of entity clients with interests that diverge from those of the constituent, any oral or written representations made by the attorney regarding the representation, the person to whom the attorney's services were billed and who in return paid these bills, and the presence of independent counsel for the constituent.''[36]

One of the corporate lawyer's tasks during the incorporation process is to draft the pertinent documents. These documents may include, for example, the articles of incorporation, by-laws, stock transfer restrictions, employment agreements, and shareholder agreement. While documents such as the articles of incorporation and corporate bylaws may not give rise to an individual's reasonable expectation of being separately represented by the drafting attorney, the situation may become more problematic where the lawyer drafts documents that set forth the rights and interests of individual shareholders. Such documents may include buy-sell agreements, voting agreements, and employment contracts. Presumably, the attorney drafts such documents with the corporation's best interests in mind. One may ponder, however, whether the individuals, especially those who have had prior significant interactions with the attorney, have a reasonable expectation that the attorney is simultaneously protecting their personal best interests.[37]

Having been deemed to be concurrently representing an individual constituent in addition to the organization may place the attorney in a precarious position. As clients, they are all owed the duties of loyalty and confidentiality.[38] If the attorney in fact is representing each of these common clients, then that attorney evidently is further bound by the obligations relating to intermediaries.[39] For example, in a situation where an

**36.** Comment, *supra* note 33, 106 Harv. L. Rev. at 691.

**37.** *Id.* at 691–704.

**38.** *See* Model Rules 1.6, 1.7.

**39.** Model Rule 2.2. Note that the 2002 amendments to

attorney is rendering legal advice to two clients who are organizing a business enterprise, the attorney is likely to be serving as an intermediary.[40]

ABA Model Rule 2.2 sets forth obligations assumed by an attorney serving as an intermediary. The attorney must consult "with each client concerning the implications of the common representation" and procure "each client's consent to the common representation."[41] This consultation requires the attorney to present to each client the advantages, disadvantages, and risks involved, including the effect on the attorney-client privilege.[42] As an intermediary, the attorney must consult with each client regarding decisions to be made, so that each client is able to make adequately informed decisions.[43] Moreover, in the event that litigation eventuates between the clients, communications between these common clients and the attorney-intermediary generally will not be shielded from discovery by the attorney-client privilege.[44] Nonetheless, the attorney's obligation of confidentiality remains intact. Thus, the attorney's communications to one common client may not be revealed (absent that client's consent) to any of the other common clients. As a result, the attorney must strike a delicate balance between keeping each client adequately informed and maintaining the requisite confidentiality.[45]

ABA Model Rule 2.2 provides that an attorney "may" act as an intermediary; thus the lawyer's potential role as an intermediary does not become an issue unless two or more clients are involved. In other words, under the Model Rules, a lawyer may not be an interme-

the Model Rules, implementing the Ethics 2000 Commission's position, deleted Rule 2.2. Revised Rule 1.7 presumably encompasses the lawyer as intermediary dilemma. Scenario III addresses in greater depth the lawyer as intermediary.

**40.** *Id.* Model Rule 2.2 cmt. 3.

**41.** *Id.* Model Rule 2.2(a)(1).

**42.** *Id.*

**43.** *Id.* Model Rule 2.2(b).

**44.** *Id.* Model Rule 2.2 cmt. 6.

**45.** *Id. See* Rollock, *Professional Responsibility and Organization of the Family Business: The Lawyer as Intermediary*, 73 Ind. L.J. 567 (1998).

diary between a client and a non-client third party.[46] Between two or more clients, however, the lawyer may serve as an intermediary when the parties have potentially conflicting interests.[47] For this reason, the attorney should seek certainty with respect to client identity. As an example, in analyzing an ambiguous attorney-client relationship, one court opined: "This court concludes that there was a joint representation which resulted in an attorney-client relationship; that the joint representation was improper and that resort to the conflict of interest rules is therefore available."[48]

In the context of a close corporation, the Model Rules attempt to clarify the standard by stating that a lawyer acts as an intermediary "in helping to organize a business in which two or more clients are entrepreneurs . . . ."[49] Whatever clarity this provision actually provides, however, depends on the presence of attorney-client relationships between the attorney-intermediary and the entrepreneur-clients. To lessen liability exposure, it would be prudent for the attorney to obtain consent from the involved parties that they are not the attorney's clients.

What steps an attorney representing a forming or just-formed closely held corporation should take to minimize potential conflicts of interest, liability exposure, and violation of the ethical rules at times are illusive.[50] One approach would be for the attorney to attempt to have all the parties involved agree that the attorney is representing only the organization, rather than the individuals. If such an agreement is reached, it should be evidenced in writing. Thus, the safest way for the attorney to avoid potential liability resulting from multiple representation is to have each constituent seek indepen-

**46.** Model Rule 2.2 cmt. 1.

**47.** *Id.*

**48.** *AVR, Inc. v. Cemstone Products, Co.*, 1993 WL 104933 at *7 (D.Minn.1993). *See also, Hansen, Jones & Leta, P.C. v. Segal,* 220 B.R. 434 (D.Utah 1998).

**49.** Model Rule 2.2 cmt. 3.

**50.** *See* Mitchell, *supra* note 18, 74 Cornell L. Rev. 466 (1989).

dent counsel. For example, language incorporated into a shareholder agreement for a closely held corporation may provide:

> "The Shareholders acknowledge that this Shareholder Agreement contains significant restrictions on their respective interests, and that they have been advised to seek their own legal counsel for themselves (and for the spouse, if any, of each individual Shareholder) and they represent and warrant that they are not represented by and are not relying on the Corporation's legal counsel for any legal advice concerning the meaning, interpretation, or legal effect of this Agreement."

However, retention of separate counsel for each shareholder is likely to make the process of organizing a business far more expensive. The constituent shareholders may well view these costs as prohibitive. Indeed, vigorous representation by separately retained counsel may "nix" the venture before it ever commences.

The following Scenario highlights some of the significant ethical issues and dilemmas an attorney faces when attempting to represent a closely held enterprise.

## SCENARIO

Ashley and Alan Beasley are first cousins. A few years back, they started a small internet dating service. At first, the business was nothing more than an entertaining past time. As the site's popularity grew, however, they became increasingly aware of its moneymaking potential. Although their dating service was offered free of charge, the site had enough daily visitors to warrant a call from a large restaurant chain inquiring about placing a banner advertisement on Ashley's and Alan's web page. They were thrilled at the proposition and the potential opportunities it presented. Before making any rash decisions, Ashley and Alan sought out professional legal advice.

The next day the two paid a visit to their old high-school friend, Buddy Buddanut, who had graduated from law school three years earlier. They explained to him their situation and asked what course of action he recommended. Since his admission to the Bar, Buddy had little experience with business planning or corporate formation; however as a long-time friend of the Beasley family, and in need of the legal fees to be generated by corporate representation, he accepted the engagement. Having recently attended a CLE program on the advantages of incorporating business enterprises, Buddy suggested they incorporate the business immediately. He explained the tremendous advantages that he had heard a corporate structure provided and the liability shield it provided to Ashley and Alan. They agreed and Buddy pulled out an incorporation forms template that happened to be on his computer. "Double A Dating Services, Inc." thereupon became a validly formed corporation after filing the required documents with the State.

After being retained, Buddy suggested that members of the board of directors be named. Ashley and Alan decided to appoint themselves and one seemingly objective party. Ashley said that her younger brother David, who had just received his M.B.A., was not too terribly busy these days, and would be happy to become a shareholding member of their board. Wanting to keep the business in the family, Alan found this agreeable. Buddy next explained the necessity of corporate bylaws, allocation of control, and dispute resolution procedures.

Ashley and Alan decided to issue 100 shares of common stock, each one taking 48 shares, and thus each having 48% control of the corporation. The remaining four shares were issued to David, who was now a part-time employee of the business. Since their positions in Double A Dating Services, Inc. were going to be full time careers, Ashley and Alan decided that they would each fully participate in the daily management and operations of the corporation.

Business went swimmingly. Several large advertising site accounts were procured and the number of "hits" on Double A's site was increasing every day. With virtually no overhead cost, Ashley and Alan were brilliantly making out. Then Alan met his soul mate and suddenly lost much of his enthusiasm for the business. Ashley, although concerned, decided to say nothing in hopes that Alan would eventually come around. Instead, he announced that he was getting married, and wanted to work no more than thirty hours a week. Ashley was now extremely concerned. Rather than assisting Ashley in making significant business decisions, Alan was spending much of his time with his fiancée.

Even without Alan's input, things continued to go smoothly for the next six months. Ashley was becoming increasingly amenable to Alan's role, or lack thereof, as it allowed her the opportunity to run key aspects of the business largely on her own. One day, Ashley was approached by Sid Savvy, who owned an online service similar to that of Double A's Dating Services. Sid asked Ashley if Double A's Dating Services would be interested in acquiring another internet dating service. Sid explained that he was ready to retire and get out of the fast-paced life of a dotcom entrepreneur, and was willing to accept $275,000 for his company. After giving the idea careful consideration, Ashley concluded that this was the best thing that could happen to the business. An affordable source of financing was readily available, and Sid's internet site, Savvy Sid's Find–A–Date, Inc., was already a legend in its own time. It was the most popular dating service in the region. Ashley called Alan to tell him the exciting news. Alan, however, was furious with Ashley for even considering such a significant proposition without consulting him.

Perplexed, Ashley asked why it would even matter to him, considering that he had relatively little involvement in the business for nearly a year. Alan told Ashley that regardless of his diminished role in key operations, he was still a 48% owner and heavily dependent on his salary from their corporation, since Double A's Dating Service did not pay shareholder dividends. Alan felt the acquisition presented too much of a financial risk to their corporation, and that Ashley wanted to grow simply for the sake of growth. He reiterated that he, not Ashley, was the Company's great visionary.

Ashley realized that Alan could use his 48% voting interest and position on the board of directors in attempts to thwart the planned acquisition. So she decided to make David her voting ally. The next stockholders' meeting was only one month away. Ashley phoned David and explained the situation. Not only did Ashley plan to defeat Alan in the vote, she also told David that it was time to remove Alan from the board and terminate his employment altogether. David agreed to go along with the plan, provided that he would receive a $3,000 monthly increase in his salary.

Ashley then called Buddy at his office. She explained to Buddy what was about to happen, and asked Buddy to do what was necessary as the Company's attorney to help effectuate Alan's removal from the board of directors and termination of his employment, due to the fact that he was no longer pulling his weight. Ashley also directed Buddy to draft a written offer by the Company to purchase Alan's 48% stock ownership at 50% of the stock's recently appraised value. Buddy, confused and a bit uneasy about being involved in a family squabble, began to carry out Ashley's requests. Ten days before the stockholders' meeting, Buddy had to attend another CLE program. The topic of this one was shareholder oppression in a close corporation. Buddy walked out with a sick feeling in his stomach. He wondered, was he about to become one of Alan's oppressors and subject not only Ashley and David but also himself to serious liability exposure?

Did Buddy act properly in initially accepting the engagement and now following Ashley's directive? What steps should Buddy undertake at this time?

*

# Scenario II

# CONFIDENTIALITY OWED TO EXISTING AND FORMER CLIENTS

Attorneys sometimes face a tension between two fundamental principles of professional conduct. Lawyers owe a duty of confidentiality to their clients, a duty that, with certain exceptions, prohibits them from "reveal[ing] information relating to [the] representation of a client."[1] But attorneys cannot assist a client "in con-

1. Rule 1.6(a) of the ABA Model Rules provides:

> "(a) A lawyer shall not reveal information relating to representation of a client unless the client consents after consultation, except for disclosures that are impliedly authorized in order to carry out the representation, and except as stated in paragraph (b).
>
> (b) A lawyer may reveal such information to the extent the lawyer reasonably believes necessary:
>
> (1) to prevent the client from committing a criminal act that the lawyer believes is likely to result in imminent death or substantial bodily harm; or
>
> (2) to establish a claim or defense on behalf of the lawyer in a controversy between the lawyer and the client, to establish a defense to a criminal charge or civil claim against the lawyer based upon conduct in which the client was involved, or to respond to allegations in any proceeding concerning the lawyer's representation of the client."

The 2002 amendments to Rule 1.6 adopted by the ABA's House of Delegates continue to preclude a lawyer from disclosing client confidences to prevent the client from committing financial wrongdoing. *See generally* C. Wolfram, *Modern Legal Ethics* § 6.7 (1986).

duct that the lawyer knows is criminal or fraudulent."[2] The tension between these rules often arises when an attorney believes that he has a duty to remain silent regarding a client's representation, but also is concerned that such silence may facilitate a client's fraudulent or criminal act. What an attorney must, cannot, or may do or disclose in any situation may largely depend on (1) whether the client has ceased the criminal/fraudulent activity or such activity is ongoing and/or contemplated, and (2) whether the client has already used the attorney's work product to commit a crime or fraud or if the client is currently using or in the near future plans to use the lawyer's work to perpetuate the improper activity. Moreover, the rules in this area vary widely by jurisdiction.

The issue of disclosure becomes further complicated when the attorney's client is an organization, such as a corporation. Because a corporation is an artificial entity, it must act through its duly authorized constituents. Thus, if an attorney learns that an officer or employee of a corporate client is engaging or is about to engage in fraudulent activity, the attorney must ascertain whether such person is acting on behalf of or independently from the corporation. In this situation, Model Rule 1.13 directs the attorney to "proceed as is reasonably necessary in the best interest of the organization" including, if warranted, "referring the matter ... to the highest authority that can act in behalf of the organization as determined by applicable law."[3]

By bringing the potential fraud to light within the company, the attorney may be able to prevent it and

**2.** Model Rule 1.2(d). Rule 1.2(d) states: "A lawyer shall not counsel a client to engage, or assist a client, in conduct that the lawyer knows is criminal and fraudulent, but a lawyer may discuss the legal consequences of any proposed course of conduct with a client and may counsel or assist a client to make a good faith effort to determine the validity, scope, meaning or application of the law."

**3.** *Id.* Model Rule 1.13(b). The highest authority within the organization ordinarily is the board of directors or similar governing body.

thus save the corporate client from liability. Although the attorney may communicate with constituents of the corporation (such as directors, shareholders and employees) in connection with learning about the potential fraud, she will be limited in terms of what information she may share with the constituents, particularly if their interests are adverse to the corporate client. As a comment to Rule 1.13 states, the "lawyer may not disclose to such constituents information relating to the representation except for disclosures explicitly or implicitly authorized by the organizational client in order to carry out the representation or as otherwise permitted by Rule 1.6." Thus, when communicating with constituents associated with an organizational client, the business lawyer must be able to distinguish between those acting in their organizational capacity on behalf of the company and those acting in their personal constituent capacity, and must disclose confidential information relating to her representation of the client only to the former.

When a client, whether an individual or organization, during the course of a lawyer's active representation of that client uses or plans to use the attorney's work to perpetrate a fraud, the ABA Model Rules permit the lawyer to withdraw from the representation.[4] Indeed, when continued representation will result in a violation of applicable law or ethical rules, the attorney must withdraw.[5] The attorney also may cease representation if the client has used the "lawyer's services to perpetrate a crime or fraud."[6] Given that an attorney may withdraw from representing a client when the lawyer's services are used to perpetrate an ongoing or completed fraud or crime, a key issue thus becomes how much "noise" ("noisy" withdrawal) the attorney can make in terminating the representation—that is, what can or should the attorney do or say to indicate that the client has acted or will act fraudulently or illegally? For example, may the lawyer disaffirm a legal opinion she

**4.** *Id.* Model Rule 1.16(b).

**5.** *Id.* Model Rule 1.16(a)(1).

**6.** *Id.* Model Rule 1.16(b)(2).

rendered based on materially false information provided by her client? By disaffirming a previously issued legal opinion and making such a "noisy" withdrawal, a likely collateral consequence is the disclosure, inferentially, of information that relates to the representation that otherwise comes with the protection of Model Rule 1.6 as a client confidence. "Unlike a silent, unexplained withdrawal, a lawyer's explicit dissaffirmance of work product [such as a legal opinion] prepared by the lawyer in the course of the representation, may well be understood as amounting to a representation by the lawyer that the client information on which the disaffirmed document relied is untrustworthy, thereby necessitating the withdrawal."[7]

The American Bar Association (ABA) Committee on Ethics and Professional Responsibility has issued an opinion on this subject, concluding that "[w]hen a lawyer's services have been used in the past by a client to perpetrate a fraud, *but the fraud has ceased*, ... a 'noisy' withdrawal is not permitted."[8] Nonetheless, many states disagree with the ABA position and allow counsel to make a "noisy" withdrawal when the client used such lawyer's services to commit a now-completed fraud or crime.[9]

Even in those jurisdictions adhering to the ABA's position, the issue remains as to how an attorney should balance the tension between maintaining client confidences and preventing a client from committing a fraud. Moreover, this tension is not limited to situations where a lawyer is currently representing a client. Because an attorney's duty of confidentiality extends to *former*

**7.** *See* ABA Comm. on Ethics and Professional Responsibility, *Withdrawal When a Lawyer's Services Will Otherwise Be Used to Perpetrate a Fraud,* Formal Op. 92–366 (1992) (setting forth the limited instances in which an attorney may "disaffirm documents prepared in the course of the representation that are being, or will be, used in furtherance of [a] fraud, even though such a 'noisy' withdrawal may have the collateral effect of inferentially revealing client confidences").

**8.** *Id.*

**9.** *See* discussion *infra* notes 22–30 and accompanying text.

clients,[10] a lawyer faces the issue of what information regarding a former client he may disclose to third parties, including the former client's successor counsel, when the attorney knows or reasonably believes that the client is perpetrating a fraud or crime using work product that the lawyer had prepared for the client in the now-terminated representation.

As a general principle, the ABA Model Rules strongly favor an attorney maintaining her silence both during and subsequent to the representation, regardless of whether the lawyer terminated a current representation under Model Rule 1.16 or the representation ended on its own terms.[11] Indeed, Model Rule 1.6(b)(1) permits the lawyer to reveal client confidences only "to the extent the lawyer believes necessary to prevent the client from committing a criminal act that the lawyer believes is likely to result in imminent death or substantial bodily injury."[12] By not permitting attorney disclosure of client confidences in "noisy" withdrawal situations (such as where only financial loss is at issue), the ABA Committee asserts that the lawyer take such action only to the extent required to prevent use of such lawyer's work product in connection with the former client's criminal

**10.** See Model Rule 1.6 cmt. 22 ("The duty of confidentiality continues after the client-lawyer relationship has terminated.").

**11.** See *id.* Model Rule 1.6 cmt. 16 (2000) ("After withdrawal the lawyer is required to refrain from making disclosure of the client's confidences, except as otherwise provided in Rule 1.6.").

**12.** The 2002 amendment to Rule 1.6(b)(1) provides: "A lawyer may reveal information relating to the representation of a client to the extent the lawyer reasonably believes necessary to prevent reasonably certain death or substantial bodily harm." Note that, as proposed by the ABA's Ethics 2000 Commission, Model Rule 1.6(b) would have been expanded to broaden the grounds on which a lawyer may disclose a client's confidences when such client has used the lawyer's services to commit a fraud. Under this proposal, disclosure is permitted to prevent a client's ongoing or future fraudulent activity that likely will result in substantial injury to another's financial interests as well as to rectify past financial injury. This proposal has not been adopted to date by the ABA's House of Delegates.

or fraudulent conduct.[13]

For example, consider the situation in which a lawyer represents a client for a specific business transaction. Suppose that during the transaction, the client fraudulently used the attorney's work product to commit a financial fraud unknown to the attorney. The business lawyer, upon later finding out about the fraud, may wish to disaffirm the documents she prepared so as to disassociate herself from the client's improper conduct. As noted above, if the fraud has ceased, the attorney under the ABA's approach cannot disaffirm the work product.[14] But what if the documents prepared by the attorney are used by the client to maintain an ongoing fraudulent transaction—for example, to obtain loans from a bank under a fraudulently obtained line of credit? The question the business lawyer faces is whether the continued use of the documents constitutes a basis that would allow the attorney to disaffirm the documents.

The ABA Committee on Ethics and Professional Responsibility in Formal Opinion 92–366 has addressed this issue, and the strong differences between the formal opinion and the dissent illustrate the difficulties that a business lawyer may face in determining the appropriate course of action. At the heart of the matter was a one-year old opinion letter that an attorney had drafted as part of a loan closing and that the bank presumably still relied upon in administering a line of credit established by the transaction. The loan, the attorney's opinion, and financial statements used in the loan all were

**13.** *See* ABA Op. 92–366, note 7 *supra* (stating that "in disaffirming her work product the lawyer should take only such steps as are reasonably necessary to accomplish the intended purpose of preventing use of her work product in the client's fraud"). Note, however, as discussed *supra* note 7 and accompanying text, the making of a "noisy" withdrawal will often inferentially result in the disclosure of client confidences otherwise protected under Model Rule 1.6.

**14.** *Id.*

premised on false and altered contracts created by the client's chief executive officer and treasurer.[15]

The majority opinion concluded that the attorney's withdrawal from representation in the client's matters involving the bank may not be sufficient to prevent the attorney from assisting the former client in committing fraud. Instead, the attorney may be required to disaffirm her opinion letter in order to make the withdrawal effective. Hence, "where the client avowedly intends to continue to use the lawyer's work product, this amounts to a *de facto* continuation of representation even if the lawyer has ceased to perform any additional work. The representation is not complete, any more than the fraud itself is completed."[16] But formally disaffirming previous work should be considered a measure of last resort. As an alternative, the attorney could inform the client's new counsel "that she can no longer stand behind" the documents that the attorney had prepared.[17] The ABA opinion notes, however, that the "lawyer may and indeed must decline to discuss or otherwise reveal anything about the disaffirmed work product beyond the simple fact that she no longer stands behind it."[18]

In their dissent to the opinion, three members of the ABA Committee specifically challenged the majority's conclusion that a previously terminated representation continues if the former client is still using the attorney's work product to perpetuate a fraud.[19] The dissent contended that the majority ignored the plain meaning of the Model Rules by turning a past-completed representation into a present one. The dissent concluded

**15.** The CEO and treasurer, as well as the third member of the Board of Directors who was not involved in the fraud, agreed with the attorney to cease creating fraudulent contracts, but would not agree to inform the bank or other third parties of their previous fraudulent conduct. *See id.*

**16.** *Id.*

**17.** *Id.*

**18.** *Id.*

**19.** The dissent opined that the majority was "compelled to resort to an act of linguistic prestidigitation: an old opinion letter is transformed into a current representation whenever it is used."

that the majority's opinion might expose attorneys to disciplinary and civil liability for resurrected past representations,[20] including the possibility of liability for failing to disaffirm the work product of a previous representation.[21]

As noted at the outset of this Scenario, the rules governing an attorney's duty of confidentiality vary by jurisdiction and also may expand the grounds on which an attorney may or must disclose client confidences. Notably, the American Law Institute's (ALI) Restatement of the Law Governing Lawyers permits (but does not require) an attorney to disclose client confidences to prevent, rectify, or mitigate substantial financial loss, even if the fraud has already taken place.[22] Even more

**20.** "If a dead representation is resurrected by the client's decision to use old work product, that result presumably obtains for proper non-fraudulent use of work product as well. What duties does the lawyer owe to the revived client during this second representation period? What if the lawyer does not know the client is using the old work product? ..." *Id.* (dissent).

**21.** "Presumably, therefore, if [requiring the attorney to disaffirm the opinion letter] is a duty, and tied to effective mandatory withdrawal under Model Rule 1.16(a)(1), the lawyer's failure to disaffirm documents would be an occasion of disciplinary action against her." *See id.* (dissent).

**22.** ALI, *Restatement of the Law Governing Lawyers* § 67 (2000), which provides in part:

"§ 67. Using or Disclosing Information to Prevent, Rectify, or Mitigate Substantial Financial Loss

(1) A lawyer may use or disclose confidential client information when the lawyer reasonably believes that its use or disclosure is necessary to prevent a crime or fraud, and:

(a) the crime or fraud threatens substantial financial loss;

(b) the loss has not yet occurred;

(c) the lawyer's client intends to commit the crime or fraud either personally or though a third person; and

(d) the client has employed or is employing the lawyer's services in the matter in which the crime or fraud is committed.

(2) If a crime or fraud described in Subsection (1) has already occurred, a lawyer may use or disclose confidential client information when the lawyer reasonably believes its use or disclosure

significant, many states pursuant to their ethical rules permit or mandate disclosure of client fraud. Likewise, certain states, such as Michigan,[23] Pennsylvania,[24] and Virginia,[25] permit an attorney under certain conditions to disclose client confidences to rectify financial harm. As stated in the ALI's Restatement of the Law Governing Lawyers:

> "A small minority of the states [have] adopted the ABA Model Rules' approach, strictly limiting disclosure as recommended by the ABA. However, most jurisdictions—currently, 42—have ... included substantial financial injury (or variant, but similar language) as a ground for permissible disclosure, in addition to substantial bodily harm."[26]

is necessary to prevent, rectify, or mitigate the loss."

**23.** Mich. Rules of Prof. Conduct, Rule 1.6(c)(3) ("A lawyer may reveal ... confidences and secrets to the extent reasonably necessary to rectify the consequences of a client's illegal or fraudulent act in the furtherance of which the lawyer's services have been used").

**24.** Penn. Rules of Prof. Conduct, Rule 1.6(c)(2) ("A lawyer may reveal such information to the extent that the lawyer reasonably believes necessary ... to prevent or to rectify the consequences of a client's criminal or fraudulent act in the commission of which the lawyer's services are being or had been used").

**25.** Va. Rules of Prof. Conduct, Rule 1.6(b)(3) (Attorneys may reveal a client confidence that "clearly establishes that the client has, in the course of representation, perpetrated upon a third party a fraud relating to the subject matter of the representation").

**26.** ALI, *Restatement of the Law Governing Lawyers, supra* note 22, § 67, at 514. *See* G. Hazard & W. Hodes, *The Law of Lawyering*, App. 4, at 1259–1266 (2d ed. 1990 & 1994 supp.). *See also*, N. Crystal, *Professional Responsibility—Problems of Practice and the Profession* 404–420 (1996); S. Gillers, *Regulation of Lawyers* 609–621 (6th ed. 2002); G. Hazard & W. Hodes, *The Law of Lawyering* (3d ed. 2001); A. Kaufman, *Problems in Professional Responsibility* 207–221, 283–303 (3d ed. 1989); T. Morgan & R. Rotunda, *Professional Responsibility—Problems and Materials* 288–294 (7th ed. 2000); J. Noonan & R. Painter, *Professional and Personal Responsibilities of the Lawyer* 128–177 (2d ed. 2001); D. Rhode & D. Luban, *Legal Ethics* 226–241 (3d ed. 2001); R. Zitrin & C. Langford, *Legal Ethics in the Practice of Law* 189–190 (2d ed. 2001).

Thus, for example, in Texas, "[a] lawyer may reveal confidential information . . . when the lawyer has reason to believe it is necessary to do so in order to prevent the client from committing a criminal or fraudulent act . . . [or] to the extent revelation reasonably appears necessary to rectify the consequences of a client's criminal or fraudulent act in the commission of which the lawyer's services had been used."[27] Under these various state rules, as distinguished from the ABA's position, the attorney representing the client who fraudulently obtained a loan (see above) would be allowed to disclose the fraud underlying the loan as a means of rectifying the consequences of the fraud.[28]

As another example, whereas Model Rule 1.6(b) permits disclosure only to prevent a client from committing a crime that may result in death or substantial bodily harm, the New Jersey rule broadens the rule to *require* an attorney to reveal client confidences not only when the client's criminal, illegal, or fraudulent act would result in death or substantial bodily harm, but also when the client's actions are "likely to result in . . . substantial injury to the financial interest or property of another."[29] Also consider New York, which specifically addresses the issue of withdrawing previous opinions that may still be relied upon by a third party. In New York, a "lawyer may reveal . . . [c]onfidences or secrets

**27.** Texas Rules of Prof. Conduct, Rule 1.05(c)(7)–(8). Various Texas rules "indicate the underlying public policy of furnishing no protection to client information where the client seeks or uses the services of the lawyer to aid in the commission of a crime or fraud." *Id.* cmt. 10.

**28.** Further note that under the Texas rule, an attorney does *not* have a *duty* to disclose the fraud. *See id.* cmt. 14 ("Although preventative action is permitted by paragraphs (c) and (d), failure to take preventative action does not violate those paragraphs").

*See generally* Langevoort, *Where Were the Lawyers? A Behavioral Inquiry Into Lawyers' Responsibility for Clients' Fraud,* 46 Vand. L. Rev. 75 (1993); Painter & Duggan, *Lawyer Disclosure of Corporate Fraud: Establishing a Firm Foundation,* 50 SMU. L. Rev. 225 (1996).

**29.** N. J. Rules of Professional Conduct, Rule 1.6(b)(1).

to the extent implicit in withdrawing a written or oral opinion or representation previously given by the lawyer and believed by the lawyer still to be relied upon by a third person where the lawyer has discovered that the opinion or representation was based on materially inaccurate information or is being used to further a crime or fraud.''[30]

Regardless of these various state rules permitting disclosure of client confidences, some states have not moved in this direction. The State Bar of California Standing Committee on Professional Responsibility and Conduct, for example, in addressing the issue of what an attorney can and should do in light of a client's fraud, has stated that the lawyer is prohibited from disclosing anything regarding the fraudulent activity without the client's consent. The attorney, however, must try to persuade the client from furthering the fraud. If the client persists in the misconduct, the lawyer must withdraw from the representation.[31]

Attorneys need to keep in mind that disclosure requirements are not established solely by professional ethics; by appearing in certain forums, a business lawyer may become subject to a distinct set of obligations. For example, the Securities and Exchange Commission (SEC) takes the position that a lawyer ''engages in 'unethical or improper professional conduct' . . . when a

**30.** N.Y. Lawyer's Code of Prof. Resp. DR 4–101(c)(5). *See also*, DR 7–102(b)(1) (''A lawyer who receives information clearly establishing that . . . [t]he client has, in the course of the representation, perpetrated a fraud upon a person or tribunal shall promptly call upon the client to rectify the same, and if the client refuses or is unable to do so, the lawyer shall reveal the fraud to the affected person or tribunal, except when the information is protected as a confidence or secret.''); R. Simon, *Simon's New York Code of Professional Responsibility Annotated* (2000).

**31.** *See* State Bar of Cal. Standing Comm. on Prof. Responsibility and Conduct, Formal Op. 1996–146 (1996). *See also,* Cal. Bus. and Prof. Code § 6068(e) (''It is the duty of an attorney . . . to maintain inviolate the confidence, and at every peril to himself or herself to preserve the secrets, of his or her client'').

lawyer with significant responsibilities in the effectuation of a company's compliance with the disclosure requirements of the federal securities laws becomes aware that his client is engaged in a substantial and continuing failure to satisfy those disclosure requirements, his continued participation violates professional standards unless he takes prompt steps to end the client's non-compliance.''[32] Such steps include counseling the client to make corrective disclosure. It may be necessary for the attorney to inform the corporation's board of directors of this problem. If remedial action is not effected by the client, then counsel must resign in order not to be co-opted in the client's fraud.[33] Moreover, pursuant to the Sarbanes–Oxley Act of 2002, the SEC must promulgate a rule

> "(1) requiring [a subject] attorney to report evidence of a material violation of securities law or breach of fiduciary duty or similar violation by the company or any agent thereof, to the chief legal counsel or the chief executive officer of the company (or the equivalent thereof); and
>
> (2) if the counsel or officer does not appropriately respond to the evidence (adopting, as necessary, appropriate remedial measures or sanctions with respect to the violation), requiring [such] attorney to report the evidence to the audit committee of the board of directors of the issuer or to another committee of the board of directors comprised solely of directors not employed directly or

**32.** *In the Matter of Carter and Johnson*, [1981 Transfer Binder] CCH Fed. Sec. L. Rep. ¶ 82,847, at 84,172 (SEC 1981).

**33.** *Id.* at 84,172–84,173. The SEC's position at this time appears consistent with the ABA Model Rules although the Commission has not recently opined on whether counsel has discretion or is obligated to reveal the client's fraud to third parties. *Id.* at 84,173 n. 78. *See generally* Dolin, *SEC Rule 2(e) After Carter–Johnson: Toward a Reconciliation of Purpose and Scope,* 9 Sec. Reg. L.J. 331 (1982); Gruenbaum, *Clients' Frauds and Their Lawyers' Obligations,* 68 Geo. L.J. 191 (1979).

indirectly by the issuer, or to the board of directors.''

Much of the preceding discussion has focused on what may be considered as exceptions to the general rule of confidentiality owed to clients. Thus, if a lawyer resigned from representation of the client due to the client's fraudulent activity and wishes to disclose the former client's previous fraud, the lawyer would need to search for some basis within her jurisdiction's professional rules of ethics (or related commentary) to justify the disclosure of confidential information. This might lead some attorneys to believe that it may be best, and certainly ethically acceptable, if they were to keep knowledge of any previous or continuing fraud to themselves.

Nonetheless, an attorney may not be able to pursue an ''ostrich'' approach toward a client or former client's fraudulent activity in the name of preserving its confidences. Consider, for example, *In re O.P.M. Leasing Services, Inc.*,[34] involving a law firm that, after learning of its role in closing one fraudulent transaction for a client, received assurances from the client's principals that they would not commit any further fraud. The law firm continued to close fraudulent transactions for the client despite ''numerous additional facts ... that should have raised suspicions about the bona fides of'' the transactions.[35]

Although the law firm subsequently terminated its representation as outside general counsel, it agreed to mischaracterize the termination as a mutual decision

**34.** *In re O.P.M. Leasing Services, Inc.* (1983) (Bankruptcy Trustee Report). *See also, In re O.P.M. Leasing Services, Inc.*, 40 B.R. 380 (Bkrtcy.S.D.N.Y. 1984); G. Hazard, S. Koniak & R. Cramton, *The Law and Ethics of Lawyering* 304–310 (3d ed. 1999); S. Taylor, ''Ethics and the Law: A Case History,'' *N.Y. Times Magazine* at 31 (Jan. 9, 1983).

**35.** O.P.M. Bankruptcy Trustee Report, *supra* note *34*, at 359. *See id.* at 372 (considering these ''red flags,'' the attorneys ''should have proceeded with extreme caution'' in closing the financings).

between the firm and client.[36] After the law firm's resignation, the former client continued to close fraudulent transactions using either in-house counsel or another law firm that were oblivious regarding the actual reasons for the original law firm's resignation.[37]

The law firm's conduct in *O.P.M.* "raise[d] issues beyond professional ethics.... No rule of professional ethics can or should exempt lawyers from the general legal proscriptions against willful blindness to the clients' crimes or reckless participation in them."[38] Or, to put the issue another way, "a lawyer is not privileged to unthinkingly permit himself to be co-opted into an ongoing fraud and cast as a dupe or a shield for a wrong-doing client."[39] When the client involved is a former client, however, the questions that were raised above in the ABA opinion once again resurface. If, presumably, an attorney should not remain idle as a wrong-doing former client continues to use the attorney's work product to conduct a fraud, should the attorney be entitled to disclose confidential information related to the fraud? The answer to this dilemma, as seen from the discussion above, depends to a large extent on the ethical rules of the applicable jurisdiction.

This dilemma leads to another question: What should an attorney do when the former client's prospective successor counsel calls to find out why she stopped representing the client. A useful measure is to reply, "I am unable by the ethical rules of professional conduct to explain why I resigned unless the former client gives me permission to tell you." This statement, on its face, merely restates the general principle contained in the

**36.** *See id.* at 399 (stating that the law firm retained two law professors to counsel it on the ethical issues involved). *See also, id.* at 378–379 (The trustee also noted the close relationship between the law firm and the client, including that the law firm received up to 65% of its revenues from the client and that one of the attorneys served on the client's board of directors.).

**37.** *Id.* at 417–421.

**38.** *Id.* at 423.

**39.** *Carter and Johnson*, 1981 WL 384414, [1981 Transfer Binder] CCH Fed. Sec. L. Rep. ¶ 82,847, at 84,172.

Model Rules and protects the former client's confidences. But it also should alert the prospective successor counsel to ask the client to grant permission for the predecessor counsel to discuss the representation. If the client refuses to give such permission, that should signal the prospective successor counsel that the client may be doing something unethical, and, accordingly, should prompt such counsel to decline the representation.[40]

Let us now consider how the above issues play out in the following Scenario.

## SCENARIO

David Benedict has built up a successful finance company, Benedict Financing, Inc., in which he helps consumers and small businesses finance the acquisition of or the lease of household appliances, office equipment and related furnishings. He is dedicated to improving his community and through his business has established a reputation as the most decent, caring, and honest businessperson in Plattensburg Oaks.

After Benedict Financing's longtime outside legal counsel retired and moved to Florida, David retained Oscar McMurray as outside counsel. Although he is more than 20 years Oscar's senior, David considers Oscar the brother he never had. Oscar used to be David's next-door neighbor and paperboy, and worked at Benedict Financing during high school and college. For Oscar's college graduation present, David paid Oscar's first year of law school tuition.

After many years in the business, David decided to retire so that he and his wife Clarissa could travel. David sold the business to his daughter Susan's husband, Pete Pistel, and gave up his seat as the Company's sole director to Pete. Unable to let go of the business he built up from scratch completely, however, David retained 5% stock ownership and an option to buy

40. *See* Brown, *Counsel With a Fraudulent Client,* 17 Rev. Sec. Reg. 913 (1984); Steinberg, *Attorney Liability for Client Fraud,* 1991 Colum. Bus. L. Rev. 1, 21–22 (1991).

back from Pete an additional 20% of the Company's stock.

Unfortunately, Pete had neither David's business acumen nor his ethics. As the business began to falter, Pete tried to obtain a loan using the Company's finance leases as collateral, but was unable to secure the financing. Getting desperate, Pete took the form lease that Oscar had previously developed for Benedict Financing and used it to alter several existing leases and to forge false leases. Based on these fraudulent documents, Pete obtained a loan for Benedict Financing from an out-of-town lender seeking to establish itself in Plattensburg Oaks. Oscar provided an opinion letter for the transaction after reviewing the leases. Because they all conformed to the form lease he developed, Oscar believed that the leases were valid. In addition to the loan, Pete subtly nudged David into exercising his option to repurchase from Pete 20% of the stock in the Company. When David examined the fraudulent financial statements that Pete had prepared in connection with the loan closing, he decided to buy back the stock, not knowing that the financial statements were materially false.

With the loan proceeds in hand, Pete was able to keep the business barely surviving. He realized, however, that he would eventually need another loan. To make the Company appear profitable, over a period of several months, he forged additional leases. The pressure of keeping the business going started to get to Pete, and he began to drink heavily. One night about a year after the original loan, Pete had too much to drink at a gathering of David's family and friends to celebrate Clarissa's birthday. He inadvertently told Oscar about the fraudulently obtained loan. Oscar confronted him the next day when Pete was sober. Pete admitted his role in the previous fraudulent loan transaction but not to forging any leases since then. When Oscar said that he did not think he could represent Benedict Financing anymore, Pete told Oscar that he was working on another transaction with the lender, which had agreed to loan the Company more money and extend the debt, and asked Oscar to help him close the deal. Oscar said that he would not do any work in connection with closing the deal, but would stay on as outside general counsel for a short transition period. Pete also asked Oscar not to tell David anything about Pete's behavior because "it would break David's heart."

One day a few weeks later, after Oscar had concluded his representation of Benedict Financing, Oscar returned to his office after lunch. He checked his voice mail and found a message from the successor counsel that Pete retained to close the loan transaction. The attorney indicated that she was curious why Oscar was not closing the loan for Benedict Financing since he had been so well connected with the Company. The next voice mail message was from David, who found out that Oscar had terminated his representation of the Company and wanted to know why. David concluded his message: "Oscar, if there is something going on at my Company, I need to know and I trust you to tell me about it."

How should Oscar respond?

*

# Scenario III

# THE LAWYER AS INTERMEDIARY

Elsewhere in this text, we consider the ethical issues facing an attorney who desires to simultaneously represent multiple clients in the business (or transactional) setting.[1] An attorney in this context will be challenged to aptly satisfy the obligations owed, including the duties of confidentiality and loyalty, to each client. In these situations, the Model Rules permit a lawyer to represent multiple clients in the business context where the parties' interests potentially may conflict. In undertaking such representation, the lawyer may be viewed as serving as an intermediary between two or more clients, playing more of a counseling role to facilitate the desired arrangement or transaction rather than ardently pursuing the interests of each client.[2]

The Model Rules spell out the conditions in which an attorney may serve as an intermediary.[3] Key ele-

**1.** *See, e.g.*, Scenarios I, V, and VI herein.

**2.** *See* Model Rules of Professional Conduct, Rule 2.2 cmt. 1 ("A lawyer acts as an intermediary under this Rule when the lawyer represents two or more parties with potentially conflicting interests."); *Id.* Rule 2.2 cmt. 8 ("The consultation [between the lawyer and the clients] should make clear that the lawyer's role is not that of partisanship normally expected in other circumstances.").

**3.** *Id.* Rule 2.2 provides:

"(a) A lawyer may act as intermediary between clients if:

(1) the lawyer consults with each client concerning

ments are: consent from all clients after thorough consultation, the attorney's reasonable belief that all clients' best interests can be served, and the attorney's reasonable belief that she can be impartial. In addition, Model Rule 2.2 requires that the attorney reasonably believe that the clients can make adequately informed decisions and obliges the lawyer to consult with each client regarding decisions to be made and their implications.

The Ethics 2000 Commission, as adopted in the 2002 amendments to the Model Rules, deleted Rule 2.2. Nonetheless, Rule 2.2 serves as a useful benchmark to assess the propriety of the lawyer as intermediary. The provisions of Rule 2.2 and its commentary therefore continue to be helpful in our analysis of counsel's role in this setting. Moreover, considerations relating to the lawyer as intermediary are now contained in the Comments (*see, e.g.*, Comments 28–33) to Model Rule 1.7.

the implications of the common representation, including the advantages and risks involved, and the effect on the attorney-client privileges, and obtains each client's consent to the common representation;

(2) the lawyer reasonably believes that the matter can be resolved on terms compatible with the clients' best interests, that each client will be able to make adequately informed decisions in the matter and that there is little risk of material prejudice to the interests of any of the clients if the contemplated resolution is unsuccessful; and

(3) the lawyer reasonably believes that the common representation can be undertaken impartially and without improper effect on other responsibilities the lawyer has to any of the clients.

(b) While acting as intermediary, the lawyer shall consult with each client concerning the decisions to be made and the considerations relevant in making them, so that each client can make adequately informed decisions.

(c) A lawyer shall withdraw as intermediary if any of the clients so requests, or if any of the conditions stated in paragraph (a) is no longer satisfied. Upon withdrawal, the lawyer shall not continue to represent any of the clients in the matter that was the subject of the intermediation."

As noted in Rule 2.2's commentary, a "lawyer acts as intermediary in seeking to establish or adjust a relationship between clients on an amicable and mutually advantageous basis."[4] Two situations, for example, in which this may occur in the transactional setting are organizing a business between two or more entrepreneurs and undertaking a financial reorganization of an entity in which two or more clients have an interest.[5] Factors that impact whether intermediation is appropriate in a given situation include: the likelihood of reducing the legal costs that otherwise would be incurred if the parties were each represented by separate counsel,[6] how amicable or contentious the parties' relationship is,[7] the degree of compatibility of the parties' interests,[8] whether the lawyer subsequently will represent the parties on a continuing basis, and "whether the situation involves creating a relationship between the parties or terminating one."[9] In other words, intermediation may be appropriate where the parties are best able to work together to achieve the mutual benefits associated with the contemplated arrangement or transaction. To the extent that the relationship has or may turn more confrontational, the clients often are better served by procuring independent legal representation.

The lawyer serving as an intermediary entails significant consequences.[10] Certainly, client confidentiality

**4.** *Id.* Rule 2.2 cmt. 3.

**5.** *Id.* The role of the lawyer as intermediary in the close corporation setting is addressed in Scenario I herein.

**6.** *See id.* Rule 2.2 cmt. 1 (a key indicia demonstrating an intermediary relationship is if the parties share responsibility for the lawyer's fee), cmt. 3 (separate counsel may lead to additional costs).

**7.** *See id.* Rule 2.2 cmt. 4 ("a lawyer cannot undertake common representation of clients between whom contentious litigation is imminent or who contemplate contentious negotiations").

**8.** *See id.* Rule 2.2 cmt. 5 (one appropriate form of intermediation is "where the clients' interests are substantially though not entirely compatible").

**9.** *Id.*

**10.** *See id.* Rule 2.2 cmt. 8 ("In acting as intermediary between clients, the lawyer is required to consult with the

is a paramount concern. An attorney "acting as intermediary requires a delicate balance" between providing client A with sufficient information for A to make adequately informed decisions and protecting client B's confidences, and vice versa.[11] If A and B have an open and amicable relationship such that they freely exchange important information with respect to the subject matter at issue, counsel will more aptly balance each client's need-to-know while preserving the other's secrets. But the attorney's ability to balance these interests becomes precarious when B refuses to reveal confidential information to A and such information materially impacts key aspects of the contemplated arrangement or transaction. In such a situation, the lawyer may be compelled to terminate her role as intermediary.[12]

Moreover, if litigation subsequently arises between the parties, a related consequence is the probable loss of the attorney-client privilege. Under the prevailing view, the attorney-client privilege ordinarily does not protect communications between commonly represented clients and their attorney.[13] The commentary to Model Rule 2.2 cautions "it must be assumed that if litigation eventu-

clients on the implications of doing so, and proceed only upon consent based on such a consultation. The consultations should make clear that the lawyer's role is not that of partisanship normally expected in other circumstances."). *See generally Klemm v. Superior Court*, 142 Cal.Rptr. 509 (Cal.App.1977); N. Crystal, *Professional Responsibility—Problems of Practice and the Profession* 392–400 (1996); G. Hazard, S. Koniak & R. Cramton, *The Law and Ethics of Lawyering* 627–628 (3d ed. 1999); D. Rhode & D. Luban, *Legal Ethics* 473–477 (3d ed. 2001); Dzienkowski, *Lawyers as Intermediaries: The Representation of Multiple Clients in the Modern Legal Profession*, 1992 U. Ill. L. Rev. 741 (1992); Rollock, *Professional Responsibility and Organization of the Family Business: The Lawyer As Intermediary*, 73 Ind. L.J. 567 (1998).

**11.** *See* Model Rule 2.2 cmt. 6 (citing to Model Rules 1.4 *Communication* and 1.6 *Confidentiality of Information*).

**12.** *See id.* ("If the balance cannot be maintained, the common representation [i.e., intermediation] is improper.").

**13.** *See id.* ("With regard to the attorney-client privilege, the prevailing rule is that as between commonly represented clients the privilege does not attach.").

ates between the clients, the [attorney-client] privilege will not protect any such communications, and clients should be so advised."[14] Hence, unavailability of the attorney-client privilege further highlights the need for circumspection when determining whether counsel should serve as intermediary.

Another important consequence of using intermediation is its tenuous nature. The status of the attorney as intermediary may be quite fragile and susceptible to termination.[15] For example, any client may terminate the relationship by demanding that the attorney withdraw from the representation.[16] Moreover, if any of the conditions precedent necessary for establishing the intermediary relationship cease to exist, that too will terminate the relationship. Thus, (1) if the parties' relationship becomes less amicable and significantly more contentious, (2) if the lawyer does not believe the matter can be resolved in the clients' best interests, or (3) if the attorney no longer can be impartial—any of those events, among others, will necessitate termination of the intermediation.[17] Finally, if the intermediation is terminated, the lawyer must walk completely away from the matter, as the Model Rules forbid her from representing any party in the matter thereafter.[18]

**14.** *Id. See FDIC v. Ogden Corp.*, 202 F.3d 454, 460 (1st Cir.2000) (applying Massachusetts law) ("[W]hen a lawyer represents multiple clients having a common interest, communications between the lawyer and any one (or more) of the clients are privileged as to outsiders but not *inter sese*."); S. Gillers, *Regulation of Lawyers* 307 (6th ed. 2002).

**15.** *See* Model Rule 2.2(c). Moreover, according to Rule 2.2 cmt. 9: "Where the lawyer is intermediary, the clients ordinarily must assume greater responsibility for decisions than when each client is independently represented."

**16.** *Id.* Rule 2.2(c) & cmt. 10.

**17.** *See id.* & cmts. 4, 7, 10.

**18.** *Id.* Rule 2.2(c). For an example of a state ethical rule requiring that the attorney disclose the implications of the intermediation in writing and that the affected clients consent in writing, see Colorado Rules of Prof. Conduct, Rule 2.2(a). *See generally* American Law Institute, *Restatement of the Law Governing Lawyers* §§ 122, 130 (2000).

Let us consider the issues that a lawyer may face in acting as an intermediary using the following Scenario.

## SCENARIO

Lana Lazaras received a phone call from her client, Sarah Safar, asking Lana to meet her at the country club. Lana has known Sarah since high school and has been her primary business attorney for approximately 15 years. During that time, Sarah has built up a property management company ("SPMCo") from scratch and has become one of the most prominent businesspersons in the community.

When Lana arrived, Sarah was sitting with Bennie Belonger, Sarah's brother-in-law. Bennie moved to town approximately five years ago and has been working primarily as a business consultant. Lana was recommended to Bennie by Sarah and has performed some legal work for him, successfully helping him with respect to some real estate investment partnerships. After Lana joined her clients at the table, Sarah announced that she was going to sell her property management company to Bennie. They had already reached an agreement on the fundamental terms of the transaction (including price and structure) and wanted Lana to draft the documents necessary to complete the transaction. The following is an excerpt of their conversation.

Sarah: We've already agreed on the price, the payment terms, and everything else. All we need from you, Lana, is to put the paperwork together.

Bennie: We're also going to split your bill 50–50. Sarah has spoken highly of you ever since I came to town, and you did a great job helping me on those real estate investments. We know that you'll be able to get the work done quickly and reasonably.

Lana: Sarah, why are you selling?

Sarah: Well, um, I just decided that I want to enjoy life more. With [my daughter] Sally going to college next year, [my husband] Sammy and I want to do more traveling.

Lana: What about you, Bennie? Do you know anything about running a property management company?

Bennie: Not specifically, but I do know how to market and grow a business, and I have a few ideas along those lines. Besides, Sarah tells me that the guy in her office, Chris Castlebaum, has been managing the daily matters for her for the last few years. So, I'll make it worth his while to run the business for me.

Lana: What are you going to do—bring him in as an equity partner?

Bennie: I might down the road, but I'll start with a nice raise. I like the guy, and I think we can have a good working relationship.

Sarah: In fact, I originally talked to Chris about his buying the Company, but he's not in a financial position to do that now.

Lana: Well, it does not sound like it should be any problem for me to do this work. But I should talk with the two of you about some of the implications of me representing both of you at the same time. First of all, I am required by professional ethics to maintain each of your confidences and . . .

Sarah: Lana, you know that I think "legal ethics" is an oxymoron. You don't need to talk to us about confidences and the like. Bennie and I have been very open and frank in negotiating this deal, and I think we're both comfortable with the process.

Bennie: I've seen the Company's financials, tax returns, budgets, everything. She's seen my income tax returns and net worth. We're okay on all that.

Lana: Well, fine, as long as you don't think there will be a problem.

Following the meeting, Lana started drafting the necessary documents for the transaction. She also assigned an associate of her firm, Allan Nussbaum, to complete a due diligence review of SPMCo's corporate documents and management contracts. Lana previously had either drafted or reviewed all the relevant documents, so she assumed that Allan would not have a difficult time following a due diligence checklist that she prepared for him. With checklist in hand, Allan trudged off to SPMCo's offices. Sarah was out of the office, so Chris Castlebaum put Allan in a conference room with all the necessary documents.

When Lana arrived at her office the next morning, Allan was waiting to talk with her. "I wasn't sure if I should tell you this, but I decided I should," Allan started. "I was at SPMCo's offices pretty late last night, and Chris Castlebaum was the only other person there. We decided to order some pizza, and when we went into his office to get a phone book, he had a picture on his desk of him and Sarah in—well, let's say a very friendly position. When he saw that I saw the picture, he fell into his chair and started crying. He told me how they had gotten really close. He told her about a month ago that he loved her, but she said that she couldn't go on anymore cheating on her husband. That's why she's selling the business, out of guilt or something like that. Anyway, he said that without her, there's nothing keeping him in this town and that his brother could help him get a great job in Chicago. So, he said he's probably going to move there."

Lana was floored by this information. She thanked Allan for his superb work and for telling her the information. She also asked that he not tell anyone, even in the firm, about what he found out; Allan said he would keep quiet.

Later on that day, Lana arranged for Sarah to come over to her house that evening on the pretense of discussing some of the documents necessary for the sale. When Sarah arrived and sat down, Lana asked her about her affair with Chris. Sarah asked, "How do you know?" Lana told her about Allan's conversation with Chris. "Don't worry, I asked him not to tell anyone else," Lana finished. "But we do have to discuss what we're going to do about this."

Sarah: What do you mean, "what we're going to do about this?" It's over—*we* are not going to do anything.

Lana: Sarah, I understand that you do not want this to get out, but it puts me in a difficult situation. The fact that Chris is probably going to leave the Company is something that Bennie would want to know.

Sarah: Bennie can't know. If he did, he would tell Sammy and my marriage would be a real mess. You're my lawyer and my friend. You're not supposed to tell my secrets to anyone. You're the one always throwing your professional ethics in my face. Well, now I'm going to hold you to them: I forbid you to tell Bennie about this!

Focusing on Lana's decision whether to accept the intermediation arrangement and the facts as they developed, what were and are Lana's options?

*

# Scenario IV

## CORPORATE INTERNAL INVESTIGATIONS: WHAT ABOUT CONFIDENTIALITY?

An attorney's ability to render effective legal advice largely depends on the client's willingness to provide detailed and truthful information. Absent such candor, it frequently becomes impractical for the attorney to conduct a meaningful analysis of the client's possible legal rights and remedies. Toward that end, Model Rule 1.6 recognizes the essentiality of the client providing truthful information to his attorney.[1] Rule 1.6 generally protects from revelation confidences and secrets of the client (including communications coming within the attorney-client privilege). As the commentary to the Model Rules explains, the protection of "confidential information of the client not only facilitates the full development of facts essential to proper representation of the client but also encourages people to seek early legal assistance."[2] The principle of lawyer-client confidentiality encourages the client "to communicate fully and frankly with the lawyer even as to embarrassing or

**1.** Model Rules of Prof. Conduct, Rule 1.6. Rule 1.6 is addressed at length also in Scenario II.

**2.** *Id.* Rule 1.6 cmt. 2.

legally damaging subject matter."[3]

In the context of organizational representation, the principle of lawyer-client confidentiality (and the specific communications it protects) becomes more complex. When retained to represent an entity, the attorney's professional duties generally run only to that entity, and not to the constituents through whom the entity communicates.[4] Generally, corporate clients receive the same level of protection of confidentiality as an individual client; however, difficulty arises due to the fact that the corporation must speak through its constituents.[5] Since it is the constituents who must speak on behalf of the organization, communications between the organization's attorney and the organization (through the constituents) must receive some level of protection in order for the organization to benefit from the attorney-client privilege.

The Supreme Court examined the degree of protection these communications should receive in the landmark *Upjohn* case.[6] In its analysis, the Court focused more on the subject matter of the communications and less on the particular organizational constituent from whom the communications were made.[7] As the Court explained, "[t]he communications concerned matters within the scope of the employees' corporate duties, and the employees themselves were sufficiently aware that they were being questioned in order that the corporation could obtain legal advice."[8] As a result, the Court reasoned, "[c]onsistent with the underlying purposes of the attorney-client privilege, these communications must be protected against compelled disclosure."[9] Thus, the Supreme Court held that, while the constituents

**3.** *Id.* Rule 1.6 cmt. 4.

**4.** *Id.* Rule 1.13. For further discussion on this topic, see Scenarios I, II, VI, IX herein.

**5.** Mulroy & Thesing, *Confidentiality Concerns In Internal Corporate Investigations*, 25 Tort & Ins. L.J. 48, 49 (1989).

**6.** *Upjohn Co. v. United States*, 449 U.S. 383 (1981).

**7.** *Id.* at 394.

**8.** *Id.*

**9.** *Id. See* J. Gergacz, *Attorney–Corporate Client Privilege* (2d ed. 1990).

themselves were not in an attorney-client relationship with the corporation's attorney, their communications on behalf of the corporation were nevertheless protected by the privilege existing between the corporation and the corporation's attorney.[10]

Hence, the attorney-client privilege protects subject communications from compelled disclosure to an outside third party. Consequently, the *Upjohn* decision ultimately deals with the degree to which the attorney-client privilege protects communications made on behalf of an organizational client by the organization's constituents. The situation becomes more ambiguous, however, with respect to whether such communications also are

**10.** The *Upjohn* Court also addressed the work product doctrine's application to documents prepared in connection with employee interviews conducted by an attorney during an internal investigation. To the extent that these documents reflect privileged communications, they are protected by the attorney-client privilege. To the extent that these documents reflect the mental impressions of the attorney conducting the interview, they are protected by the work product doctrine. *Id.* at 401. The Court did not, however, grant an absolute privilege to work product documents; rather it held that the moving party is required to make a sufficient showing of necessity and unavailability in order to compel disclosure. *Id.* at 402.

In *Hickman v. Taylor*, 329 U.S. 495 (1947), the Supreme Court recognized the work product doctrine, which was subsequently codified in Rule 26 of the Federal Rules of Civil Procedure. The work product doctrine ultimately protects from compelled discovery tangible items that are prepared "in anticipation of litigation or for trial" (FRCP 26(b)(3)). Essentially, the doctrine has been interpreted to protect a lawyer's mental impressions and legal analysis. In conducting an internal investigation, attorneys will inevitably keep written records of information gathered during employee interviews. To prevent these tangible items from being subject to future discovery, commentators have suggested that the attorney should attempt to mix as many mental impressions and legal analyses as possible among the acquired and recorded information. *See* Kenny & Mitchelson, *Corporate Benefits of Properly Conducted Internal Investigations*, 11 Ga. St. L. Rev. 657, 667 (1995). *See also*, *Redvanly v. NYNEX Corp.*, 152 F.R.D. 460, 466 (S.D.N.Y. 1993) (holding that the corporation's attorney's notes were discoverable because they were "a running transcript of the meeting" and failed to reflect the attorney's mental impressions).

protected from disclosure to other constituents within the organization. This issue may arise, for instance, in the context of an internal investigation within an organization.[11]

Internal investigations can assist an organization's management in ascertaining the advantages and disadvantages of certain corporate policies.[12] In other instances, internal investigations may be aimed at uncovering suspected wrongful and/or criminal acts perpetrated by certain company employees during the course of employment.[13] In such a situation, the internal investigation can take on paramount importance in the corporation's attempt to fend off or minimize the imposition of criminal or serious civil sanctions as a result of the wrongful acts.[14]

Internal investigations generally are comprised of two courses of action: a document review and employee interviews.[15] It is in the area of employee interviews that the investigating attorney particularly must exercise caution with respect to representations (or the lack

**11.** *See generally* Cohn, *The Organizational Client: Attorney–Client Privilege and the No–Contact Rule*, 10 Geo. J. Leg. Eth. 739 (1997); Hamilton, *Conflict Disparity and Indecision: The Unsettled Corporate Attorney–Client Privilege*, 1997 Ann. Surv. Am. L. 629 (1997); Kenny & Mitchelson, *supra* note 10, 11 Ga. St. L. Rev. at 663–667; Leslie, *The Costs of Confidentiality and the Purpose of Privilege*, 2000 Wis. L. Rev. 31 (2000); Rice, *Attorney–Client Privilege: The Eroding Concept of Confidentiality Should Be Abolished*, 47 Duke L.J. 853 (1998); Thornburg, *Rethinking Work Product*, 77 Va. L. Rev. 1515 (1991); Zacharias, *Harmonizing Privilege and Confidentiality*, 41 S. Tex. L. Rev. 69 (1999); Zornow & Krakur, *On the Brink of a Brave New World: The Death of Privilege in Corporate Internal Investigations*, 37 Am. Crim. L. Rev. 147 (2000).

**12.** *See* Kenny & Mitchelson, *supra* note 10, 11 Ga. St. L. Rev. at 661.

**13.** *See* Mulroy & Thesing, *supra* note 5, 25 Tort & Ins. L.J. at 48.

**14.** For discussion on the role internal investigations play in helping an organization avoid criminal liability, *see* Valukas & Stauffer, *Internal Investigations Of Corporate Misconduct*, 6 Insights No. 2, at 17 (Feb. 1992).

**15.** *See* Kenny & Mitchelson, *supra* note 10, 11 Ga. St. L. Rev. at 665–667.

thereof) made to the individual employee. This is especially true where the individual employee's interests appear adverse to the interests of the organization.[16]

While Model Rule 1.13 states that the attorney's loyalty is solely to the organizational client, the rule also obliges the attorney to "explain the identity of the client [namely, the organization] when the lawyer knows or reasonably should know that the organization's interests are adverse to those of the constituents with whom the lawyer is dealing."[17] An internal investigation designed to uncover possible employee wrongdoing may place the organization's interests and certain employees' interests at odds, thereby potentially invoking the attorney's Rule 1.13(d) obligation to explain the identity of the client to the interviewee-employee.[18]

As discussed above, one of the main objectives of the privilege is to encourage the corporate client to speak freely and candidly with its attorney.[19] In conducting an internal investigation, the attorney should seek to obtain as much truthful and factual information as practicable.[20] In order to do so, it may be necessary, or at least advantageous, for the employees with whom the attorney speaks to presume that their communications to the attorney are not only protected from disclosure to outside third parties, but also are confidential with respect to other constituents within the organization.[21]

Oftentimes employees may possess material information pertaining to the attorney's fact-finding investi-

**16.** *See* Model Rule 1.13.

**17.** *Id.* Rule 1.13(d).

**18.** *Id.* Model Rule 1.13(d). *See* Rule 4.3 ("In dealing on behalf of a client with a person who is not represented by counsel, a lawyer shall not state or imply that the lawyer is disinterested.").

**19.** *See* discussion *supra* notes 1–10 and accompanying text.

**20.** *See e.g.* Kahn, *Preserving The Confidentiality of Internal Corporate Investigations*, 1 *J. Corp. Disclosure & Confidentiality* 155, 155–158 (1989).

**21.** *See* Aibel, *Corporate Counsel and Business Ethics: A Personal Review*, 59 Mo. L. Rev. 427, 438–439 (1994).

gation that they do not feel comfortable disclosing for fear of repercussions. If, for example, an employee had done something that could jeopardize her position within the organization, it is unlikely that the employee will share the information with the attorney, unless the employee knows, or at least thinks, that her communications are confidential and will not be disclosed even to other constituents. As counsel for the organization, the attorney is obligated to remain steadfastly loyal to the organization's best interests, and act in a manner intended to further those interests.[22]

As one source explains:

> "Counsel for the corporation owes an allegiance to the corporation as an entity rather than to the employee being interviewed. In many circumstances, the interests of individual employees may be adverse to the interests of the corporation. . . . In the interest of candor, counsel should instruct employees that he represents the corporation, that he is not their attorney, that employees cannot assert the attorney-client privilege to bar disclosure of the interview, and that the corporation possesses the attorney-client privilege but may waive it and disclose the information."[23]

Under this approach, the attorney may well be obligated to give the employee-interviewee a Miranda-style warning.[24] Indeed, in certain factual contexts, some courts have imposed liability on counsel who failed to provide sufficient notice to a non-client third party.[25]

**22.** *See* Model Rule 1.7.

**23.** Mulroy & Thesing, *supra* note 5, 25 Tort & Ins. L.J. at 62.

**24.** *See* Martin, *When Corporate Counsel Get Caught in the Middle*, Cal. Law. at 75 (Dec. 1989); Steinberg, *Attorney Liability for Client Fraud*, 1991 Colum. Bus. L. Rev. 1, 19–20 (1991); Valukas & Stauffer, *supra* note 14, 6 Insights No. 2, at 19.

**25.** *See Parker v. Carnahan*, 772 S.W.2d 151 (Tex.App.1989); *Collin County v. Johnson*, 1999 WL 994039 (Tex.App.1999). For further discussion, *see* C. Wolfram, *Ethical Considerations For Corporate Counsel: Advising And Disclosing In An Uncertain Legal World*, 796 PLI/Corp. 235 (1992).

From the organizational-client's perspective, the problem is that such a warning could result in the employee being less than truthful, thus having a chilling effect on the employee's willingness to candidly cooperate with the investigation.[26] Consequently, warning the non-client employee with respect to the consequences of making unprivileged self-incriminating statements could compromise the attorney's ability to fulfill her investigative responsibilities. In other words, the constituents may "not confide information the attorney feels is critical to competent representation."[27] It is for this very reason that disagreement prevails as to whether employee-constituents should be given a warning regarding the limits of confidentiality. As the former Executive Vice President and Chief Legal Officer of the ITT Corporation explained:

> "There has been a good deal of discussion among corporate counsel as to whether an employee should be given a 'Miranda' type warning before being questioned in an internal investigation, or if not that, be given an opportunity to consult his or her own lawyer before submitting to interrogation. I have concluded that carrying out my professional responsibility to the corporate entity requires that neither of such courses be followed. It is my task to find out what the facts are as fully and as quickly as possible. It is the obligation of an employee to respond truthfully to questions put to him by the corporation as to activities in the course of his employment for which the corporation may be held responsible, whether civilly or criminally."[28]

**26.** Pizzimenti, *The Lawyer's Duty To Warn Clients About Limits On Confidentiality*, 39 Cath. U. L. Rev. 441, 484 (1990).

**27.** *Id. See generally* Fischel, *Lawyers and Confidentiality*, 65 U. Chi. L. Rev. 1 (1998).

**28.** Aibel, *Corporate Counsel and Business Ethics: A Personal Review*, 59 Mo. L. Rev. 427, 438 (1994). *See United States v. Int'l Brotherhood of Teamsters*, 961 F.Supp. 665, 673 (S.D.N.Y.1997) (allowing an employee not provided with warning to invoke privilege would preclude counsel "from disclosing the employee's

As internal investigations are frequently initiated to uncover facts related to suspected wrongdoing within the organization, it normally is in the corporation's best interest to retain counsel to conduct the investigation in an attempt to preserve the privileged status of any detrimental information.[29] In order to avoid potential ethical and malpractice issues, the investigating attorney in this setting ordinarily should avoid individual representation of an organizational constituent-employee. As counsel for an individual employee, the attorney will be bound by additional confidentiality obligations to that employee.[30] Therefore, prior to conducting employee interviews, prudent counsel should consider if a "Miranda-type" warning is appropriate. As one court held, "[i]n the absence of any advice by [corporate counsel] to the contrary, defendants were justified in believing that [corporate counsel] were there to protect their individual interests as well as those of the corporation."[31] Hence, a key objective of providing a "Miranda-type" warning is to avoid any appearance that the attorney somehow misled the individual employee to believe that the attorney represented such employee's personal interests as opposed to those of the corporation.[32]

Once the attorney decides that such a warning should be given to the employee, the next question is what should the warning contain? Tension exists be-

communications ... thus thwarting the investigation.").

**29.** As one source explains, "[t]he best method of ensuring that the results of the investigation remain within the company's control is to conduct the investigation in a manner specifically designed to maintain both the confidentiality of the investigative results and the attorney-client or work product privileges associated with them." Kenny & Mitchelson, *supra* note 10, 11 Ga. St. L. Rev. at 663–664.

**30.** *Id.* at 666.

**31.** *United States v. Hart*, 1992 WL 348425 at *2 (E.D. La. 1992).

**32.** *See, e.g., Westinghouse Electric Corp. v. Kerr–McGee Corp.*, 580 F.2d 1311 (7th Cir. 1978) (holding that the employees' communications to the corporation's attorney were privileged and confidential based on the reasonable belief that they were being individually represented by the corporation's attorney).

tween providing sufficient information to the employee to render the warning effective, without deterring the employee from providing accurate and truthful information. For example, the attorney simply could inform the employee that she is the lawyer for the corporation. Alternatively, counsel could tell the employee that she represents the corporation, not the employee individually, and as such, nothing that the employee says to her need be kept confidential within the organization.

The following Scenario highlights some of the ethical considerations facing an attorney conducting an internal investigation on behalf of an organizational client.

## SCENARIO

As a child, Tim Eddy loved to travel with his father who worked as a technical support analyst for amusement parks. Eddy always knew that one day he would own his very own amusement park, and it would attract visitors from all over the globe. At the age of 30, he received his break. A heavy-hitter investor by the name of Josh Willy had heard of Eddy and decided to provide the needed capital to get the park (named Eddy–Willy Amusement Park, Inc.) off the ground. Eddy, it turned out, was a natural when it came to amusement park operations. Within five years, the park was generating $20 million in annual revenues. At that time, although not publicly traded, the Company had 87 shareholders, with Eddy and Willy each owning 26% of the stock.

The most popular ride was the Sumo Tsunami. It was a huge tsunami wave that would catapult the riders several feet in the air, and then allow them to come crashing down with a giant splash. Eddy designed the ride himself and knew that it had to be operated with precision in order to avoid accidents. The only drawback to operating the ride was that in order to ensure safety, the operator's control booth had to be placed within the reach of the tsunami's incredible force. As a result, every time the wave came down, the operator was inundated with a water wall that left him/her drenched. For the first few months after the ride's inception, Eddy insisted that he operate the controls himself to make sure nothing went wrong. As business grew, however, Eddy had to spend more time attending to Company-related matters. Eddy realized the time had come to hire several people to be responsible for operating the Sumo Tsunami. For the next two years, the park was extremely successful, and the Company's board of directors began inquiring into the possibility of opening another amusement park.

Then things took a turn for the worse. The operators of the Sumo Tsunami were becoming increasingly disgruntled with their job. The constant battering they took under the huge wave proved to be more than any of them could psychologically bear. As a result, their performance began to suffer, and accidents began to occur. While none of the accidents were catastrophic, rumors were rampant within the Company. Eddy and the board of directors realized that they needed to act, and fast.

Eddy suggested hiring an outside consulting firm to figure out what the source of the problem was. The board of directors (advised by legal counsel), however, realizing that if there was some rogue element within the organization, it could lead to serious liability in the event of a lawsuit. Whatever information was uncovered thus should be sought to be kept confidential. So they suggested hiring a law firm to conduct an internal investigation. Eddy, having heard that lawyers were rogue elements themselves, was not overly enthused with the idea, but acquiesced in order to help maintain confidentiality over any information uncovered.[33]

The Company's board of directors retained a law firm that specialized in amusement park litigation to conduct the internal investigation. Before commencing,

**33.** Note that "facts" are not entitled to protection under the attorney-client privilege. Nonetheless, disclosure of such information may well be a confidence or secret, thereby implicating Model Rule 1.6. *See* Scenario II herein.

the lawyers met with the board members to mutually agree on a specific course of action. The board directed that as many employees as possible should be interviewed by counsel and that, to avoid raising suspicion that might thwart the investigation, counsel should not only focus on the Sumo Tsunami operators. Furthermore, the board wanted the employees to be as truthful as possible, and if that meant allowing them to think that their conversations with the lawyers were completely confidential, that was just fine.

The lawyers explained that since the investigation's purpose was to uncover potential wrongdoing by employees, there was a strong chance that certain employees' interests would become adverse to those of the corporation, in which case the lawyers would be ethically obligated to tell any such employee that he/she is not being represented individually by the interviewing lawyer. Upon hearing this, Eddy became agitated and responded, "Listen, we are paying you guys a ridiculous amount of money to do a really simple task, so you will tell our employees exactly what we want you to tell them, understood?" The lawyers assured Eddy that they would "do their best" to avoid saying or doing anything that would risk compromising their ability to successfully conduct the investigation.

Then the employee interviews began. First, the lawyers started with the roller-coaster operators, then moved onto the Ferris wheel, and then felt the time was right to interview the Tsunami operators. The first two interviews were almost disappointing, as the employees seemed no different than any of the other operators. The third interview, however, changed the tone of the entire investigation. This operator told the lawyers how he, and several of the other Tsunami operators felt like second-class operators because of the location of their control booth. Being right under the path of the wave, they were bombarded all day by the very waves they were creating. This employee told the lawyers that some of the operators' "friends" would come to watch them on the job, just to get a laugh when the wave came crashing down, knocking the operator out of the chair and into the padded wall that had been erected immediately behind the control booth. When asked why there was a padded wall there, the lawyers were told that it was to keep the operators from being carried away by the tremendous force of the wave.

The fourth and fifth interviews went about the same as the third interview. The sixth, however, really got interesting. This operator, Jessica Hendry, initially attempted to deny the story told by the previous operators, but after the lawyers explained that they already knew the truth, she came clean. Hendry, however, not realizing that the lawyers had only heard part of the truth, continued into uncharted territory. She said, "Well, if you guys already know all this, and I guess if you're a bunch of lawyers you can't tell anyone what we tell you, yeah, we operators decided to try to cause a few wrecks." The lawyers could not believe their ears. They were so carried away with what they had just heard that all they could think about was getting more information.

Hendry then saw Ivan Inglas, a fellow Tsunami operator, walking by. She called him over and said, "These guys are some lawyers that want to hear about our little pact to cause wrecks on the Tsunami. They have to keep their mouths shut about what we tell them."

Feeling sort of relieved about finally being able to express his resentment towards his job, Inglas began to tell his story. Just then, however, the lawyers were hit with the implications of what Hendry had said about their vow of secrecy. They decided to end the interview immediately, and told the two employees that they would get back to them as soon as possible. The lawyers realized they were in a predicament and needed time to meet with the other attorneys to explain what had happened and figure out what to do. They knew they would have to tell the other lawyers exactly what had transpired and what had been communicated during the employee interviews. But they were also aware that their actions, or lack thereof, may have jeopardized the entire investigation.

In light of the above developments, did counsel act appropriately? What actions should now be taken by counsel in continuing the investigation?

*

# Scenario V

# PARENT—SUBSIDIARY RELATED PARTY TRANSACTIONS

Attorneys who are hired by a business enterprise may have more than just one entity as their client. The parent corporation may have numerous subsidiaries that will direct their legal work to the attorney's law firm. In most dealings, this multiple representation will not pose a problem, as the interests of the subsidiaries normally will be aligned with those of the parent. The parent corporation and its subsidiaries, however, may engage in transactions between themselves. Although such related party transactions are not prohibited, they raise potential pitfalls that could trap the unwary business lawyer. Not only must the attorney properly advise his clients—both the parent and subject subsidiary—so that they comply with the law, he must fulfill his own ethical obligations.

In terms of the lawyer's professional obligations, the Model Rules of Professional Conduct demand loyalty to a client.[1] To this end, the Model Rules generally prohibit a lawyer from representing a client whose interests are directly adverse to another client or if a significant risk exists that the lawyer's representation

**1.** *See* Model Rules of Prof. Conduct, Rule 1.7 cmt. 1 ("Loyalty and independent judgment are essential elements in the lawyer's relationship to a client.").

would be materially limited by the lawyer's responsibilities owed to another present (or former) client, a third party, or the lawyer's own interest.[2] Attorneys may undertake an otherwise prohibited dual representation if they *reasonably* believe that their representation will be competent and diligent to each client *and* each client "gives informed consent, confirmed in writing."[3]

Given the above, counsel should be cautious when requested to represent both parent and subsidiary corporations in a self-dealing transaction.[4] Two basic inquiries should be made by counsel. First, are the interests of the parent and subsidiary directly adverse to each

**2.** Model Rule 1.7 provides:

"(a) Except as provided in paragraph (b), a lawyer shall not represent a client if the representation involves a concurrent conflict of interest. A concurrent conflict of interest exists if:

(1) the representation of one client will be directly adverse to another client; or

(2) there is a significant risk that the representation of one or more clients will be materially limited by the lawyer's responsibilities to another client, a former client or a third person or by a personal interest of the lawyer.

(b) Notwithstanding the existence of a concurrent conflict of interest under paragraph (a), a lawyer may represent a client if:

(1) the lawyer reasonably believes that the lawyer will be able to provide competent and diligent representation to each affected client;

(2) the representation is not prohibited by law;

(3) the representation does not involve the assertion of a claim by one client against another client represented by the lawyer in the same litigation or other proceeding before a tribunal; and

(4) each affected client gives informed consent, confirmed in writing."

**3.** *Id.* Rule 1.7(b) & cmts. to Rule 1.7.

**4.** A self-dealing transaction in this context generally is defined as the parent corporation, due to its control and domination over the subsidiary, receives a benefit to the detriment and exclusion of the subsidiary and its minority shareholders. *See Sinclair Oil Corp. v. Levien*, 280 A.2d 717 (Del.1971).

A related party transaction in this context generally is a transaction between the parent corporation and its subsidiary which may or may not be viewed under the applicable corporate law as a self-dealing transaction.

other, which would give rise to the proscription set forth in Model Rule 1.7(a)(1)? Second, do the responsibilities that the attorney owes to one client, such as the parent company, materially limit the lawyer's ability to represent the subsidiary, thereby implicating Model Rule 1.7(a)(2)? For example, if the lawyer's primary relationship is with the parent, can she effectively also represent the subsidiary in a self-dealing transaction, such as a cash-out merger whereby the subsidiary's public shareholders would be eliminated?

Even if the attorney determines that she cannot ethically represent both entities in a corporate self-dealing transaction, she may face pressure to do so. For example, the executive officers in the parent corporation may be opposed to hiring a second law firm to represent the subsidiary due to apprehension that retention of more lawyers will further complicate and impede the "deal." The officers might even threaten to terminate entirely the relationship with the attorney and her law firm unless she represents both sides. Along the same lines, the attorney may be reluctant to bring in a second full-service law firm fearing that the other firm will take away some or all of the client's future business. Furthermore, the attorney may want the revenue that she would receive from both clients and thus be willing to minimize her ethical obligations.[5] Professional responsibility, however, dictates that the attorney must hold firm against these pressures.

When a lawyer is involved in a transaction between a parent and subsidiary, his ethical responsibilities become highly intertwined with the substantive corporate law rules governing such dealings. In addition to being concerned about his own behavior, the business lawyer also must provide advice with respect to his client's conduct to assist such client's officers and directors in fulfilling their fiduciary duties to the affected corpora-

**5.** *See* Rule 1.7 cmt. 10 ("The lawyer's own interest should not be permitted to have an adverse effect on representation of a client.").

tion and shareholders.[6] With this in mind, let us first review some of the substantive law governing related party or self-dealing transactions and then examine relevant implications for an attorney's ethical duties.

In the context of parent-subsidiary self-dealing transactions, courts tend to examine the decisions made by a subject corporation's board of directors with more scrutiny than the normally deferential business judgment rule would allow.[7] Most notably, in Delaware (the most popular state where "large" publicly-held companies opt to incorporate), such transactions must meet the standard of *entire fairness*, with the burden of persuasion falling on the defendants.[8] The standard of entire fairness has two components—fair dealing and fair price—that must be assessed given the pertinent facts and circumstances involved; even though the two components may be analyzed separately, they should not be bifurcated when concluding whether the entire fairness standard has been met.[9]

The concept of fair price seems straightforward. It "relates to the economic and financial considerations of the proposed [transaction, such as a] merger, including all relevant factors: assets, market value, earnings, future prospects, and any other elements that affect the

**6.** *See, e.g.*, R. Clark, *Corporate Law* §§ 3.4–4.2 (1986).

**7.** *See A Handbook of Basic Law Terms* 27 (B. Garner ed. 1999) (defining the business judgment rule as "[t]he presumption that in making business decisions not involving direct self-interest or self-dealing, corporate directors act on an informed basis, in good faith, and in the honest belief that their actions are in the corporation's best interest").

**8.** *See Kahn v. Tremont Corp.*, 694 A.2d 422, 428 (Del. 1997) ("Ordinarily, in a challenged transaction involving self-dealing by a controlling shareholder the substantive legal standard is that of entire fairness, with the burden of persuasion resting upon the defendants."); *Weinberger v. UOP, Inc.*, 457 A.2d 701, 710 (Del. 1983) ("The requirement of fairness is unflinching in its demand that where one stands on both sides of a transaction, he has the burden of establishing its entire fairness, sufficient to pass the test of careful scrutiny by the courts.").

**9.** *See Weinberger*, 457 A.2d at 711.

intrinsic or inherent value of a company's stock."[10] Depending on the circumstances, a court could find that the duty of fair price was violated if the price itself involved in the transaction was deemed unduly low.[11]

The concept of fair dealing focuses on the process of the transaction. It "embraces questions of when the transaction was timed, how it was initiated, structured, negotiated, disclosed to the directors, and how the approvals of the directors and the stockholders were obtained."[12] The Delaware Supreme Court has noted that strong evidence of a fair process would be if both the parent and subsidiary "exerted its bargaining power against each other at *arm's length*."[13] The best way for a parent corporation and its subsidiary to arrive at an arm's length transaction is to set up a special committee of the independent members of the subsidiary's board—that is, those board members who are independent from the parent—to negotiate and approve the proposed transaction with the parent.[14]

The mere establishment of such a committee of independent directors by the subsidiary is not sufficient in and of itself.[15] The committee must in fact be indepen-

**10.** *Id.*

**11.** *See id.* at 709 (One report "show[ed] that a return on the investment at $21 [the actual purchase price] would be 15.7% versus 15.5% at $24 per share. This was a difference of only two-tenths of one percent, while it meant over $17,000,000 to the minority."); *Kahn*, 694 A.2d at 432 ("When assigned the burden of persuasion, this test [of entire fairness] obligates the directors or their surrogates to present evidence which demonstrates that the cumulative manner by which it discharged all of its fiduciary duties produced a fair transaction.").

**12.** *Weinberger*, 457 A.2d at 711.

**13.** *Id.* at 709 n.7 (emphasis added).

**14.** *Id. See* M. Steinberg, *Securities Regulation: Liabilities and Remedies* § 15.04[1] (2002); Weiss, *Balancing Interests in Cash–Out Mergers: The Promise of Weinberger v. UOP, Inc.*, 8 Del. J. Corp. L. 1 (1983).

**15.** *Kahn*, 694 A.2d at 428 ("Entire fairness remains applicable even when an independent committee is utilized because the underlying factors which raise the specter of impropriety can never by completely eradicated and still require careful judicial scrutiny.").

dent and function in that manner. Thus, there are a number of factors considered in deciding whether the subsidiary's board and/or special committee failed to satisfy their duties of loyalty and care owed to the corporation and the shareholders:

- If some directors fail to share material information among all members of the subsidiary's directors, particularly among the independent committee, in accordance with the directors' duty of candor;[16]
- If interested directors affiliated with the parent corporation exert an overbearing influence on the transaction;[17]
- If the entire transaction occurred within an unduly narrow time frame and under conditions beneficial to the parent;[18]
- If the "independent" committee members had previous significant dealings with the parent cor-

**16.** *See Weinberger*, 457 A.2d at 709–711 (failure of subsidiary board members to disclose to other subsidiary board members stock valuation information that was generated from internal subsidiary data for the benefit of the parent and to which they were privy constituted breach of fiduciary duty); *Kahn*, 694 A.2d at 431 (stating that "the Court of Chancery correctly stated that a controlling shareholder . . . must disclose fully all material facts and circumstances surrounding the transaction"). *See generally* Hammermesh, *Calling Off the Lynch Mob: A Corporate Director's Fiduciary Disclosure Duty*, 49 Vand. L. Rev. 1087 (1998); Klock, *Litigating Securities Fraud As a Breach of Fiduciary Duty in Delaware*, 28 Sec. Reg. L.J. 296 (2000).

**17.** *See Weinberger*, 457 A.2d at 710 ("Given the absence of any attempt to structure this transaction on an arm's length basis, [the parent] cannot escape the effects of the conflicts it faced, particularly when its designees on [the subsidiary's] board did not totally abstain from participation in the matter.").

**18.** *Id.* at 711 ("For whatever reasons, and they were only [the parent's], the entire transaction was presented to and approved by [the subsidiary's board] within four business days."); *Kahn*, 694 A.2d at 431 ("Initiation by the seller, standing alone, is not incompatible with the concept of fair dealing so long as the controlling shareholder does not gain financial advantage at the expense of the controlled company.").

poration to bring their "independence" into question;[19]

- If the independent committee is not advised in an adequate manner by competent, independent professionals, such as lawyers and financial advisers; moreover, these professionals should not be selected by officers of the parent or because of a previous relationship with the parent;[20] and
- If certain members of the committee fail to participate actively in the negotiation and decision-making process and/or if they overly rely on the efforts of another committee member who may not be independent.[21]

Individually, any one of these may or may not constitute unfair dealing depending on the facts of the situation. But as more of these shortcomings begin to mount, a parent corporation will have greater difficulty establishing the fairness of the transaction.

How does this substantive law interact with counsel's ethical duties? As discussed above, the primary rule of professional responsibility invoked with respect to

**19.** *See Kahn*, 694 A.2d at 426 ("Although the three [individuals] were deemed 'independent' for purposes of this transaction, all had significant prior business relationships with [the controlling shareholder] or [his] controlled companies").

**20.** *See Weinberger*, 457 A.2d at 712 ("We can only conclude from the record that the rush imposed on [the investment banker] by [the parent's] timetable contributed to the difficulties under which this investment banking firm attempted to perform its responsibilities. Yet, none of this was disclosed to [the subsidiary's] minority."); *Kahn*, 694 A.2d at 429 ("[T]he selection of professional advisors for the Special Committee doesn't give comfort; it raises questions.").

**21.** *See Kahn*, 694 A.2d at 430 (Delaware Supreme Court finding fault with one member not attending negotiations or meetings with professional advisors; a second member only partially participating; and the third member, who conducted the negotiations, being "arguably the least detached member of the Special Committee"). *See also, Kahn v. Lynch Communication Systems, Inc.*, 638 A.2d 1110 (Del.1994), *on remand*, 669 A.2d 79 (Del.1995); *Rabkin v. Olin Corp.*, 586 A.2d 1202 (Del. 1990); *Rosenblatt v. Getty Oil Co.*, 493 A.2d 929 (Del.1985).

parent-subsidiary self-dealing transactions is Model Rule 1.7. The general thrust of the rule applied to this setting is that, if an attorney cannot adequately represent both parties without significantly impairing his representation of either, such dual representation constitutes an impermissible conflict of interest. As discussed above, the initial question to consider under Rule 1.7 is whether the parent's and subsidiary's interests are directly adverse to each other. Even though both entities might benefit from a transaction between them, frequently any transaction between the two will be of a zero-sum nature: the benefit to one comes at the expense of the other. As a general proposition, the substantive law, for its part in self-dealing transactions in parent-subsidiary transactions, calls for entire fairness, including procuring competent and independent advice from professionals.[22] As a result, Rule 1.7(a) arguably prevents the same counsel from representing both parties in the negotiations.[23] But even if the parent's and subsidiary's interests are not directly adverse, the substantive law requirement that the subsidiary receive competent and independent legal advice likely means that an attorney could not fulfill that role without materially limiting his representation to the parent, or vice versa. As a result, the prohibition of dual representation in this context likely would be implicated.[24]

Even if an attorney normally would be barred from representing both parent and subsidiary due to conflict of interest, Rule 1.7 does allow the attorney to

**22.** *See supra* note 19 and accompanying text.

**23.** *See* Model Rule 1.7 cmt. 28 (stating that "a lawyer may not represent multiple parties to a negotiation whose interests are fundamentally antagonistic to each other, but common representation is permissible where the clients are generally aligned in interest even though there is some difference of interest among them").

**24.** *See generally* Symposium, *The Role of Counsel in Corporate Acquisitions and Takeovers: Conflicts and Complications*, 39 Hastings L.J. No. 3 (1988); Rotunda, *Conflicts Problems When Representing Members of Corporate Families*, 72 Notre Dame L. Rev. 655 (1997).

continue the dual representation in this setting if two elements are satisfied. First, the lawyer reasonably believes that she can render diligent and competent representation to each client, here the parent and the subsidiary.[25] In many cases, an attorney may *subjectively* believe she can properly represent both the parent and subsidiary, particularly if she has an ongoing professional relationship with both entities. But the Model Rules call for an *objective* standard—whether the lawyer "reasonably believes" that such lawyer under the circumstances would be able to provide "competent and diligent representation to each affected client."[26] The second element requires each client to give informed consent to the representation, confirmed in writing.[27] Once again, the substantive law governing corporations interacts with counsel's ethical obligations. The subsidiary would need to provide its consent independently of the parent's determination. Thus, for the lawyer to comply with her ethical duties in rendering dual representation, she should seek to ensure that the subsidiary's "independent" directors are not under the parent's domination and control.[28]

Because directors in parent-subsidiary self-dealing transactions should be particularly mindful of their fiduciary duties, counsel representing either the parent or subsidiary corporation should seek to ensure that such directors fulfill their obligations. To the extent that the attorney fails in this task—for example, if he is too driven to promote the parent company's interests and renders improper legal advice—he subjects his client and his client's directors and executive officers to liability exposure. Certainly, if counsel has acted incompetently or assisted in a fraudulent transaction, he has violat-

**25.** Model Rule 1.7(b)(1).

**26.** *Id.* & cmt. 15.

**27.** *See id.* Rule 1.7(b)(4). "Informed consent requires that each affected client be aware of the relevant circumstances and of the material and reasonably foreseeable ways that the conflict could have adverse effects on the interests of that client. . . ." *Id.* Rule 1.7 cmt. 18.

**28.** *See supra* notes 16–21 and accompanying text.

ed the Model Rules as well as being subject to liability for malpractice and aiding and abetting breach of fiduciary duty.[29]

Let us consider how these issues play out in the following Scenario.

## SCENARIO

Oneworld Corp. is a privately held holding company with interests in a variety of manufacturing and industrial businesses. Jonathan Evans founded the company and is now its Chief Executive Office (CEO) and Chairman of the Board. Evans is a very hands-on leader and demands a say in virtually every important aspect of all his businesses, including Oneworld's subsidiaries. One of his most trusted advisers is his long-term outside general counsel, Chris Mathias, who has worked with Evans for over 20 years.

Evans decides that he wants Oneworld to buy out the minority interests in one of its subsidiaries, Mac & McGaw, Inc., a farm equipment manufacturer. Oneworld already owns 51% of Mac & McGaw, with the remaining stock in the Company publicly traded on the American Stock Exchange. The value of Mac & McGaw's stock has declined over the past few years. Evans attributes this to poor weather conditions that have kept farmers from being able to afford new equipment. Believing that sales will pick up in the near future, he believes that the stock is now significantly undervalued, thus giving rise to his desire to cash-out the minority shareholders. At the time, Mac & McGaw has a nine-member Board of Directors: Evans and three other officers from Oneworld; Harold Stanley, the president of one of Mac & McGaw's suppliers; Melissa Brown, an

**29.** *See* Model Rules of Prof. Conduct, Rule 1.1 ("A lawyer shall provide competent representation to a client. Competent representation requires the legal knowledge, skill, thoroughness and preparation reasonably necessary for the representation."); Rule 1.2(d) ("A lawyer shall not counsel a client to engage, or assist a client, in conduct that the lawyer knows is criminal or fraudulent ...."). *Cf.* Rule 1.2 cmts. 9–10.

investment banker who has an existing and ongoing professional relationship with Evans and Oneworld; Francine Baker and Leonard Collins, two highly respected business people from outside companies; and Albert Anson, the Dean of the business school from a major university who also has a $60,000 a year consulting contract with Oneworld.

Evans calls Mathias over to his office and expresses his desire for Oneworld to acquire the minority interests in Mac & McGaw. Mathias suggests that Oneworld create a new subsidiary, Newco, in which Oneworld would be the sole owner and then execute a freeze-out merger in which Mac & McGaw would merge into Newco and the public shareholders of Mac & McGaw would receive cash for their stock. He advises Evans that this structure would be the easiest way to accomplish Evans' goals.

Unfortunately for Evans, he learned earlier that day that one of Oneworld's European subsidiaries requires his immediate attention and he must leave for France the next day. Prior to leaving, he tells Mathias that he is relying on him to make sure that the Mac & McGaw transaction takes place and that he will make it worth Mathias' efforts. Mathias, who is under criticism by his law partners for not being a strong rainmaker, knows that the financial reward he will receive from getting the deal done for Evans will silence some of his critics in the firm (at least for a while).

That evening, Evans and Mathias finalize their plan. They arrange for the Mac & McGaw board of directors to set up a special committee to negotiate with Oneworld. The committee is to be comprised of Stanley, Collins, and Anson. Upon making this decision, Evans expresses his approval: "Collins is too busy with his own business to get too involved in this and Anson knows where his bread is buttered. Stanley is a bit of a wild card, but should not be too much of a problem." Evans and Mathias also decide that Mac & McGaw will retain the investment banking firm of Hornsby/Wagner. Although Hornsby/Wagner has never worked for Oneworld or any of its subsidiaries, Evans knows the firm through Melissa Brown, who has a strategic alliance with that firm. Evans also tells Mathias that since he also serves as Mac & McGaw's general outside counsel, he must represent both companies in the transaction and that Evans will make sure that Mac & McGaw's board of directors signs off on that.

After hammering out those details, Evans calls in Oneworld's CFO, Denton Young. Young also serves as Mac & McGaw's treasurer and as one of its directors. The three review Oneworld's and Mac & McGaw's financials. Provided that the price of Mac & McGaw stock remains stable, they decide that Oneworld's initial offer in its negotiations with the members of the Mac & McGaw independent committee will be a 10% premium over that day's closing stock price and that Oneworld will go as high as an 18% premium if need be. They also realize that they could go as high as 25% without seriously hampering Oneworld's economic gain, but Evans rejects going that high: "We should get this done at most for an 18% premium. That's enough of a gravy train for those 'pain in the butt' shareholders."

Evans leaves for Europe the next day and expects to be gone for three weeks. He tells Mathias, "I want this done by the time I get back." Mathias immediately starts to work on the transaction: having Newco created and preparing its organizational documents; drafting the initial documents necessary for the merger transaction as Evans and he envisioned; having several phone calls with members of the Oneworld's and Mac & McGaw's boards of directors; and, of course, staying in continual contact with Evans. Ten days after Evans left, Mathias formally conveys the buy-out offer to Mac & McGaw's board of directors, which proceeds to select the pre-arranged special committee and approve Mathias as the subsidiary's counsel for the transaction. Two days later, after negotiations lasting three hours between the Mac & McGaw special committee and Oneworld, the companies issue a press release announcing the contemplated merger between Mac & McGaw and Newco whereby the Mac & McGaw minority shareholders will receive a 20% premium above market price for the cash-out of their stock in Mac & McGaw.

When Evans returns from Europe, he is irate at the premium involved in the buy-out. He screams at Mathias, "I thought I told you 18% was the top." Mathias responds, "It was Stanley. He was too much of a wild card. He kept pouring over the financials and asking for more and more, and saying that perhaps the committee should get another lawyer to get more input. It finally got to the point where I cut off how much information he was getting and forced the issue. Fortunately, we got Hornsby/Wagner to say that the 20% premium was a fair price, and I strong-armed Anson to get Collins to outvote Stanley. Otherwise, it could have been worse."

Over the next few months, Evans' predictions regarding Mac & McGaw's increasing sales come true as farmers are predicted to have bumper crops throughout most of the nation. As a result, Newco (i.e., Mac & McGaw) performs more favorably. Five months after the freeze-out merger is completed, Evans takes advantage of an eager buyer to spin off the subsidiary at a price that equates to a 45% premium above the stock price on the day that Oneworld and Mac & McGaw announced the merger with Newco. Shortly thereafter, a well-known plaintiffs' law firm locates a "representative" former minority shareholder who was frozen out in the merger. The class action lawsuit names Oneworld, Mac & McGaw (Newco), Mac & McGaw's board of directors, the investment banking firm of Hornsby/Wagner, and Mathias as defendants. In particular, Mathias is sued allegedly for aiding and abetting breach of fiduciary duty and for fraud.

What should have Mathias done to avoid this lawsuit? What arguments can he now make on behalf of his clients and himself to escape liability?

*

# Scenario VI

# THE BUSINESS LAWYER AS ADVISOR AND LITIGATOR: THE MULTIPLE REPRESENTATION DILEMMA

In many instances, it may be desirable for counsel to represent multiple clients during the course of an investigation, arbitration, mediation, trial, or administrative hearing. Indeed, from counsel's perspective, there are many benefits to representing multiple clients, such as enhancing the attorney's control over the subject proceeding (including the dissemination and collection of information), allowing for consistency in strategy, and avoiding duplication in the various efforts expended.[1] Likewise, for clients, multiple representation is cost effective, facilitates the effectuation of a "united" defense strategy, and reduces the unnecessary duplication of legal services. Despite the potential benefits, however, disadvantages also exist in multiple representation situations, including conflict of interest and ethical concerns. For example, representing multiple clients

1. *See* Brodsky & Zeena, *Multiple Representation of a Corporation and its Employees: Establishing and Protecting the Attorney–Client Privilege and Protecting Against Conflicts of Interest*, PLI No. B4–6970, 741 PLI/Corp. 175, 185 (1991); Brodsky & Zeena, *Representing a Corporation and Its Employees*, 25 Rev. Sec. & Comm. Reg. 13 (1992).

may dilute the lawyer's duty of loyalty to her clients. In other situations, the affected clients' interests may become sufficiently divergent so as to require the lawyer to withdraw from the representation.[2]

The ethical concerns of multiple representation are addressed in both The Model Code of Professional Responsibility ("Model Code") and The Model Rules of Professional Conduct ("Model Rules"). For example, Disciplinary Rule 5–105(b)–(c) of the Model Code states:

> "A lawyer shall not continue multiple employment if the exercise of independent professional judgment in behalf of a client will be or is likely to be adversely affected by the lawyer's representation of another client, or if it would be likely to involve the lawyer in representing differing interests, except . . . if a disinterested lawyer would believe that the lawyer can competently represent the interest of each and if each consents to the representation after full disclosure of the implications of the simultaneous representation and the advantages and risks involved."[3]

Similarly, Rule 1.7 of the Model Rules addresses simultaneous representation. Model Rule 1.7(a) provides:

> "Except as provided in paragraph (b), a lawyer shall not represent a client if the representation involves a concurrent conflict of interest. A concurrent conflict of interest exists if: (1) the representation of one client will be directly adverse to another client; or (2) there is a significant risk that the representation of one or more clients will be materially limited by the lawyer's responsibilities to another client, a former client or a third person or by a personal interest of the lawyer."[4]

**2.** *See* sources note 1 *supra.*

**3.** Model Code of Prof. Responsibility DR 5–105(b)–(c).

**4.** Model Rules of Prof. Conduct, Rule 1.7(a).

Under Model Rule 1.7(b), multiple representation generally is allowed if the attorney "reasonably believes that [he/she] will be able to provide competent and diligent representation to each affected client ... and each affected client gives informed consent, confirmed in writing."[5] Informed consent:

> "requires that each affected client be aware of the relevant circumstances and of the material and reasonably foreseeable ways that the conflict could have adverse effects on the interests of that client. The information required depends on the nature of the conflict and the nature of the risks involved. When representation of multiple clients in a single matter is undertaken, the information must include the implications of the common representation, including possible effects on loyalty, confidentiality and the attorney-client privilege and the advantages and risks involved."[6]

Provisions pertaining to multiple representation in the American Law Institute's Restatement of the Law Governing Lawyers essentially mirror Model Rule 1.7. One provision, for instance, provides that "a conflict of interest is involved if there is a substantial risk that the lawyer's representation of the client would be materially and adversely affected by the lawyer's own interests or by the lawyer's duties to another current client, a former client, or a third person."[7]

Although addressed in other Scenarios of this text and not the principal focus of this Scenario, there are many situations in the corporate counseling context

**5.** *Id.* Model Rule 1.7(b)(1), (b)(4). *See generally* Painter, *Advance Waiver of Conflicts*, 13 Geo. J. Leg. Eth. 289 (2000); Zacharias, *Waiving Conflicts of Interest*, 108 Yale L.J. 407 (1998); Task Force Report, *Conflicts of Interest Issues*, 50 Bus. Law. 1381 (1995).

**6.** Model Rule 1.7 cmt. 18.

**7.** American Law Institute, *Restatement of the Law Governing Lawyers* § 121 (2000). *See generally* Boyd, *Current Trends in Conflict of Interest Law*, 53 Baylor L. Rev. 1 (2001); Moore, *Restating the Law of Lawyer Conflicts*, 10 Geo. J. Leg. Eth. 541 (1997).

where multiple representation concerns exist. For example, conflicts may arise: (1) during the formation stage of an entity; (2) in situations involving closely-held enterprises; (3) in related party (such as interested director) transactions; and (4) in instances where conflicts between management and shareholders may exist, such as management self-dealing, proxy contests, leveraged buy-outs, and other alleged misconduct by management.[8] Multiple representation concerns also may arise in the litigation context. For example, potential conflicts—as illustrated by this Scenario—may arise in shareholder derivative actions and government investigations and prosecutions.

Generally, the interaction between the corporation and its divergent constituencies, including shareholders, directors and officers, may give rise to conflict dilemmas.[9] For instance, although applicable ethical provisions provide that counsel owes allegiance solely to the entity,[10] determining an appropriate course of conduct that serves the corporation's best interests may be problematic.[11] The directors, shareholders, and other constituencies affected may disagree as to the appropriate action that is in the corporation's best interests. Moreover, counsel's own assessment of the situation may be blurred by the affinity felt toward the directors and executive officers, and by the desire to defend corporate transactions which likely resulted in part from her "lawyering."[12]

**8.** *See* Bassett, *Three's a Crowd: A Proposal to Abolish Joint Representation*, 32 Rutgers L.J. 387, 418 (2001); Scenarios I, IV, V, IX herein.

**9.** *See* Elias, *Multiple Representation in Shareholder Derivative Suits: A Case-by-Case Approach*, 16 Loy. U. Chi. L.J. 613, 617 (1985). *See also*, G. Hazard & W. Hodes, *The Law of Lawyering* § 17.10 (3d ed. 2001).

**10.** *See* Model Rule 1.13.

**11.** Elias, *supra* note 9, 16 Loy. U. Chi. L.J. at 617.

**12.** *Id.* *See* C. Wolfram, *Modern Legal Ethics* 421 (1986); Landry, *Joint Representation of a Corporation and Director/Officer Defendants in Stockholder Derivative Suit: Is It Permissible?*, 18 J. Leg. Prof. 365 (1993).

Derivative suits[13] thus implicate multiple representation problems. For example, conflicts may arise when a lawyer is faced with the dilemma of representing both the corporation and its officers and directors in a derivative action. The comment to Model Rule 1.13 provides only general guidance in this context:

> "The question can arise whether counsel for the organization may defend such an action. The proposition that the organization is the lawyer's client does not alone resolve the issue. Most derivative actions are a normal incident of an organization's affairs, to be defended by the organization's lawyer like any other suit. However, if the claim involves serious charges of wrongdoing by those in control of the organization, a conflict may arise between the lawyer's duty to the organization and the lawyer's relationship with the board. In those circumstances, Rule 1.7 governs who should represent the directors and the organization."[14]

Under applicable ethical guidelines, multiple representation in derivative suits frequently is permitted so long as the client provides informed and objective consent to the representation. In the derivative action context, however, consent in many cases would be given by directors or executive officers aligned as individual defendants in the suit. Consequently, "it would be a mere charade for the same directors to vote for the corporation's consent to representation of themselves and the entity."[15] Hence, it has been suggested that, although a corporation and individual defendants theoretically may consent to dual representation, "caution [should] be exercised when applying consent provisions to the corpo-

**13.** A derivative suit is "an action brought by one or more stockholders of a corporation to enforce a corporate right or remedy a wrong to the corporation in cases where the corporation, because it is controlled by the wrongdoers or for other reasons, fails and refuses to take appropriate action for its own protection." 19 Am. Jur. 2d, *Corporations* § 2250.

**14.** Model Rule 1.13 cmt. 11.

**15.** C. Wolfram, *supra* note 12, at 426.

rate setting."[16] Additionally, Model Rule 1.13(e) provides general guidance: "If the organization's consent to the dual representation is required by [Model] Rule 1.7, the consent shall be given by an appropriate official of the organization other than the individual who is to be represented, or [such consent shall be given] by the shareholders."[17]

Although multiple representation increases the potential for conflicts in derivative suits, many courts have held that the filing of a derivative action does not necessitate separate representation.[18] Indeed, in instances where a suit is without merit, seeks minor relief, or does not allege charges of serious wrongdoing against directors or officers, counsel generally may represent both the entity and the individual defendants with their respective informed consents.[19]

In instances where derivative actions allege serious wrongdoing by management and are found to be nonfrivolous, courts have differed regarding the permissibility of multiple representation of the corporation and its representatives.[20] Early cases evidenced a certain deference to a corporation's decision to have counsel represent all parties. In *Otis & Co. v. Pennsylvania R. Co.,*[21] for example, the court concluded:

**16.** Elias, *supra* note 9, 16 Loy. U. Chi. L.J. at 617. *See Cannon v. U.S. Acoustics Corp.*, 532 F.2d 1118 (7th Cir.1976); Ass'n of the Bar of the City of New York, Comm. On Prof. Ethics, Op. No. 842, 15 The Record 80 (1960).

**17.** Model Rule 1.13(e).

**18.** *See, e.g., Schmidt v. Magnetic Head Corp.*, 468 N.Y.S.2d 649 (App.Div.1983); *Schwartz v. Guterman*, 441 N.Y.S.2d 597 (Sup.Ct.1981); *Seifert v. Dumatic Indus. Inc.*, 197 A.2d 454 (Pa.1964); C. Wolfram, *supra* note 12, at 426.

**19.** *See* sources cited note 18 *supra*.

**20.** *See, e.g., Messing v. FDI, Inc.*, 439 F.Supp. 776, 783 (D.N.J.1977); *Cannon v. U.S. Acoustics Corp.*, 398 F.Supp. 209, 220 (N.D.Ill.1975), *aff'd in part and rev'd in part*, 532 F.2d 1118 (7th Cir.1976); *Lewis v. Shaffer Stores Co.*, 218 F.Supp. 238, 240 (S.D.N.Y.1963); *Rowen v. LeMars Mut. Ins. Co.*, 230 N.W.2d 905, 917 (Iowa 1975); *Schwartz v. Guterman*, 441 N.Y.S.2d 597 (Sup.Ct.1981).

**21.** 57 F.Supp. 680 (E.D.Pa. 1944).

"[T]here is no reason to require removal of counsel as petitioned. The corporation, as an interested party having a right to appear and defend, may select such counsel as it chooses. Moreover, there is no allegation of any breach of confidence or trust of which either the corporations or the individual defendants complain."[22]

More recent decisions, however, generally favor the retention of separate counsel.[23] Indeed, some courts have expressed the view that such multiple representation is impermissible. For instance, one court stated:

> "If the same counsel represents both the corporation and the director and officer defendants, the interests of the corporation are likely to receive insufficient protection. An increased recovery for the corporation is wholly incompatible with the goal of limiting defendants' liability. Defendants' counsel is thus placed in an untenable position, and more often than not [counsel] will succumb to the pressure to approve any settlement between the shareholder and his individual clients."[24]

Multiple representation problems also may surface during government investigations, regulatory enforcement actions, and criminal prosecutions.[25] For example, potential and actual conflicts may occur in government investigations (such as the EPA, FTC, SEC, etc.) when counsel for a corporation also attempts to represent some or all of the directors, officers, and employees of the company. Likewise, conflicts may arise when counsel

**22.** *Id.* at 684.

**23.** *See, e.g., Murphy v. Washington American League Base Ball Club, Inc.*, 324 F.2d 394 (D.C.Cir.1963); *Lower v. Lanark Mut. Fire Ins. Co.*, 448 N.E.2d 940 (Ill.App.1983); *Haenel v. Epstein*, 450 N.Y.S.2d 536 (Sup.Ct.1982). *See also*, Pryor & Silver, *Defense Lawyers' Professional Responsibilities*, 78 Tex. L. Rev. 599 (2000); Note, *Disqualification of Corporate Counsel in Derivative Actions: Jacuzzi and the Inadequacy of Dual Representation*, 31 Hastings L.J. 347 (1979).

**24.** *See In re Oracle Secs. Litig.*, 829 F.Supp. 1176, 1188 (N.D.Cal.1993).

**25.** *See* C. Hazard & W. Hodes, *supra* note 9, §§ 11.12–11.13.

for a broker-dealer entity also attempts to represent subordinate officers or employees such as branch managers, supervisors, or salespersons.[26]

For example, in an SEC disciplinary proceeding, *In re Merrill Lynch, Pierce, Fenner & Smith, Inc.*,[27] the SEC's Division of Enforcement formally moved to preclude Merrill Lynch's outside legal counsel from representing the firm as well as numerous employees of the firm named as respondents in the action. The SEC argued that the close relationship between counsel, a major New York City law firm, and the brokerage firm presented actual and potential conflicts of interest to the detriment of the employee-respondents. According to the SEC, for example, Merrill Lynch could attempt to defend itself by pointing to the alleged primary culpability of, and possible concealment by, some of its employees. On the other hand, the employees could try to defend themselves by blaming management.[28]

In issuing its opinion, the administrative law judge in *Merrill Lynch* refused to preclude the law firm from representing multiple clients, stating that the SEC was unable to establish that a conflict "would necessarily occur."[29] The judge thereupon conditioned multiple representation on a procedure designed to elicit the informed consent of each employee-respondent. This procedure encompassed transmitting to each employee-respondent a copy of the judge's order, as well as the

**26.** *See* Matthews, *Effective Defense of SEC Investigations: Laying the Foundation for Successful Disposition of Subsequent Civil Administrative and Civil Proceedings,* 24 Emory L.J. 567 (1975). Mr. Matthews, a distinguished securities litigator, served as Deputy Director of the SEC's Division of Enforcement and as a partner at the prestigious firm of Wilmer, Cutler, and Pickering. He was a superb lawyer and a wonderful man.

**27.** [1973–1974 Transfer Binder] CCH Fed. Sec. L. Rep. ¶ 79,608 (ALJ 1973).

**28.** *Id.* at 83,631. *See* Matthews, *supra* note 26, 24 Emory L.J. at 579.

**29.** [1973–1974 Transfer Binder] CCH Fed. Sec. L. Rep. ¶ 79,608, at 83,631.

opportunity to read the transcript of oral arguments, briefs, and other pleadings in the case.[30]

In a more recent development, the SEC disqualified an attorney from simultaneously representing numerous persons in the same administrative enforcement proceeding.[31] Although each person consented to such multiple representation, the Commission asserted that "the right to counsel of one's choice is outweighed by the necessity of ensuring that our administrative proceeding is conducted with a scrupulous regard for the propriety and integrity of the process."[32] Hence, even though no actual conflict had yet eventuated, the SEC invoked the appearance of maintaining the integrity of its administrative process to justify disqualifying the attorney.[33]

A related issue pertaining to government investigations is determining whether separate counsel should be retained for the corporation at the outset of a government investigation. In response to this issue, an SEC Assistant General Counsel stated that, while the attorney who is asked to represent potentially conflicting parties must obtain the consent of each affected party, "one must question whether meaningful consent by the corporation is possible when in many cases there does not exist a truly disinterested management or board of directors capable of giving such consent."[34]

In the context of government investigations and prosecutions, where there often exists a commonality of interest among multiple clients, counsel and such clients may consider utilizing the joint defense doctrine.[35] Gen-

**30.** *Id.* at 83,630. *See* Matthews, *supra* note 26, 24 Emory L.J. at 579–580.

**31.** *In the Matter of Blizzard and Abel*, Investment Advisers Act Release No. 2032, 2002 WL 714444 (SEC 2002).

**32.** 2002 WL 714444 at *3.

**33.** *Id.* at *2–3.

**34.** Sonde, *The Responsibility of Professionals Under the Federal Securities Laws: Some Observations*, 68 Nw. U.L. Rev. 1, 10 (1973).

**35.** *See, e.g., United States v. McPartlin*, 595 F.2d 1321 (7th Cir.1979); *Continental Oil Company v. United States*, 330 F.2d 347 (9th Cir.1964); *Ohio–Sealy Mattress Mfg. Co. v. Kaplan*, 90 F.R.D. 21, 29 (N.D.Ill.1980); *In Matter of Grand Jury Subpoena,*

erally, the joint defense doctrine preserves the confidentiality of communications, thereby enabling parties (who are represented by one attorney or who each have retained separate counsel) to exchange otherwise privileged information in the aid of a common defense, so long as they have identical or substantially similar interests.[36] Hence, use of the joint defense doctrine may allow defendants to mount a "united front" with fewer obstacles. Specifically, in order to assert the joint defense doctrine, a party must establish three elements: "(1) There must be commonality of interest; (2) the communication must be otherwise privileged; and (3) the communication must be made in furtherance of a common defense."[37]

A well-drafted joint defense agreement[38] offers a number of advantages, including: (1) facilitating the

406 F.Supp. 381, 387–389 (S.D.N.Y.1975); Steinberg & Rogers, *The Joint Defense Doctrine in Federal Securities Litigation*, 18 Sec. Reg. L.J. 339 (1991); Uelman, *The Joint Defense Privilege: Know the Risks*, 14 Litig. No. 4, at 35 (Summer 1988); Welles, *A Survey of the Attorney–Client Privilege in Joint Defense*, 35 U. Miami L. Rev. 321 (1981).

**36.** *See also*, Moss & Bridge, *Can We Talk?: A "Steele–Y" Analysis of ABA Opinion 411*, 52 SMU L. Rev. 683, 683–684 (1999) (analyzing ABA Comm. on Ethics and Prof. Resp., Op. 98–411 (1998), which "addresses consultations with lawyers outside the consulting lawyer's firm who are not associated in the representation of this client on this matter" and opines that normally "a client-lawyer relationship does not arise between the consulting lawyer's client and the consulted lawyer [thereby] free[ing] [the consulted lawyer] of any ethical obligation [such as confidentiality] to the consulting lawyer's client").

**37.** Steinberg & Rogers, *supra* note 35, at 342. *See In Matter of Grand Jury Subpoena*, 406 F.Supp. 381, 387–389 (S.D.N.Y. 1975). *See also, In re Santa Fe Int'l Corp.*, 272 F.3d 705 (5th Cir.2001); *United States v. Zolin*, 809 F.2d 1411 (9th Cir. 1987).

**38.** In order to ensure that the privilege is available, it is advisable to enter into a written agreement or understanding with co-parties and potential co-parties before communications are exchanged. Indeed, some courts have implied that some type of formal agreement must exist before they will recognize the joint defense privilege. *See In re Bevill, Bresler & Schulman Asset Management Corp.*, 805 F.2d 120 (3d Cir.1986); *United States v. Melvin*, 650 F.2d 641 (5th Cir.1981).

flow of information and communication among attorneys, while ensuring that such information remains confidential under the attorney-client privilege and work product doctrine; (2) enhancing litigation efficiency, as the pertinent investigatory, pretrial, and trial tasks are divided among the various attorneys; and (3) enabling the multiple parties to mount a "united front" to the opposition. As with any situation involving multiple representation, however, asserting the joint defense doctrine raises potential conflicts of interest issues. In many joint defense efforts, for example, co-parties' interests may not be in complete harmony. Indeed, the very nature of litigation provides ample potential for breakdowns in communication among such co-parties.[39]

Moreover, when parties to a joint defense are each represented by individual counsel, a party may become privy to information through the joint defense that is adverse to the co-parties' interests, but advantageous to that party. Depending upon how the information is communicated, the joint defense privilege may preclude the party from using that information to the detriment of the co-parties. In such cases, cooperation with co-parties in order to present a united front may well impair the ability of one party's counsel to zealously represent the interests of the individual client. Similarly, when a single counsel represents several co-parties, compromises may have to be made in order to further the goals of the group as a whole. Any time counsel is faced with competing interests, the ability to zealously represent any one interest is diminished.[40]

Finally, a particularly troubling dilemma arises when a joint defense member defects and becomes a government witness. In this setting, the government and/or the targets (e.g., the defendants) may seek to

**39.** *See* Steinberg & Rogers, *supra* note 35, 18 Sec. Reg. L.J. at 341, 355; Capra, *The Attorney–Client Privilege in Common Representations: Information-Pooling and Problems of Professional Responsibility*, 1989 Trial Lawyer's Guide 20 (1989).

**40.** *See* Steinberg & Rogers, *supra* note 35, at 355–356.

disqualify the subject attorney(s).[41] In such event, Model Rule 1.6, which generally prohibits an attorney from revealing confidential communications, may be a cause for concern among the remaining members and their attorneys. As stated by one source:

> "[A]lthough a joint defense attorney does not have a traditional attorney-client relationship with every member of the arrangement, a duty not to reveal joint defense information or not to use such information against any member still exists. This obligation remains even if disclosure of group secrets would ultimately benefit an attorney's client. Consequently, absent other considerations, [Model] Rule 1.6 bars the attorney from cross-examining a former joint [defense] member when cross-examination would in any way reveal confidential information."[42]

In any event, it is incumbent upon counsel to disclose the potential material ramifications to his client(s) and to secure each client's written permission to engage in the joint defense. In situations where there is a realistic potential that the clients' interests may become adverse, separate counsel should be retained for each party.[43]

**41.** *See, e.g., United States v. Anderson*, 790 F.Supp. 231 (W.D.Wash.1992). In that case, the government moved to disqualify defense counsel where several of the co-workers who had entered into a joint defense agreement with the defendant subsequently became government witnesses. The court held that the circumstances at bar did not present a disabling conflict of interest that required defense counsel's disqualification.

**42.** Forsgren, *The Outer Edge of the Envelope: Disqualification of White Collar Criminal Defense Attorneys Under the Joint Defense Doctrine*, 78 Minn. L. Rev. 1219, 1243 (1994). *See Wilson P. Abraham Constr. v. Armco Steel Corp.*, 559 F.2d 250, 253 (5th Cir.1977); Solovy & Byman, *Common Interest Agreements*, Nat'l L.J., May 28, 2001, at A12.

**43.** *See United States v. Henke*, 222 F.3d 633 (9th Cir. 2000); *Ohio–Sealy Mattress*, 90 F.R.D. at 29; Levenson, *The Fading Privilege*, Nat'l L.J., May 28, 2001, at A14; Steinberg & Rogers, *supra* note 35, 18 Sec. Reg. L.J. at 356.

The following Scenario highlights many of the dilemmas that arise in the multiple representation setting.

## SCENARIO

Hywell Energy, Inc. is a multinational corporation, with its headquarters in Denver, Colorado. The Company historically generated income by purchasing and selling hard assets such as pipelines. In recent years, however, the Company has generated much of its revenue from a business described as "wholesale energy operations," including the trading of natural gas, electricity, and various other futures and commodities. The Company has been very successful; for example, during the past seven years the Company's revenues have increased from $15 billion to more than $50 billion, making it one of the premier companies in the Fortune 500.

Three months ago, Hywell Energy unexpectedly restated its earnings for the past four years, reducing the amount of earnings reported by almost $350 million, or 12%. This was necessary, according to Company spokespersons, because six unconsolidated enterprises should have been consolidated in Hywell Energy's financial statements under generally accepted accounting principles (GAAP). As a result of the announcement, the securities markets questioned the credibility of the Company, causing the price of Hywell Energy's stock to drop from around $60 a share to less than $18 in just a few months. In addition, analysts began to uncover unusual descriptions of transactions that Hywell Energy and "other entities" had entered into with a "related party" that was operated by the Chief Financial Officer of Hywell Energy, Robert Cannon. These transactions—which ultimately were revealed to be limited partnerships purportedly designed to mask the Company's debt and elevate the Company's stock price—have become the focus of investigations conducted by Congress, the U.S. Department of Justice, and the Securities and Exchange Commission.

Hywell Energy has retained Bancroft & Hood, a prestigious Chicago-based law firm which has served as the Company's outside legal counsel for decades. Additionally, the Company has agreed to pay the legal fees for Bancroft & Hood to represent 27 of the Company's employees. The executive officers, including the Chief Executive Officer, Harrison Dolan, the Chief Financial Officer Cannon, and the Executive Vice President, Charla Brier, each has retained separate counsel.

In view of these circumstances, what potential concerns face Bancroft & Hood in representing multiple clients? Where should counsel look for guidance? What disclosure should be provided by counsel to the individual defendants?

Subsequently, after receiving legal advice from their respective attorneys, all the defendants decide to execute a joint defense agreement in order to mount a "united front" against the government's investigation. Thus far, the legal strategy has been successful—the government is frustrated with how little its investigation has uncovered, and it has little probative evidence to support its allegations. Consequently, in an effort to strengthen its case, the government has made it clear that leniency, including the distinct possibility of immunity, will be accorded to any of the non-executive individual targets who come forward with significant information.

Assume that one relatively high level employee (who appears credible), Harry Easterly, comes forward and agrees to testify for the government. What are the concerns? How does it affect the remaining joint defense members who are the targets of the government's investigation? Is there a way to minimize the risk for a disqualifying conflict of interest once Easterly becomes a government witness?[44]

**44.** *See generally* Foote, *Joint Defense Agreements in Criminal Prosecutions: Tactical and Ethical Implications*, 12 Geo. J. Leg. Eth. 377 (1999); Schmitt & Hamburger, *Enron's Hiring of One Firm to Represent Forty Employees Raises Some* Concern, *Wall St. J., Jan. 29, 2002, at A6; Wilke et al.,* Two in Enron Debacle Seek Immunity Deals, *Wall St. J., Feb. 27, 2002, at A8.*

*

# Scenario VII

# SCREENING AND THE PERSONALLY DISQUALIFIED ATTORNEY

The practice of law is increasingly being dominated by "mega firms" with offices in many cities as well as foreign countries. Firms like Baker Botts, Baker and McKenzie, Foley and Lardner, Gibson, Dunn and Crutcher, Greenberg Traurig, Holland and Knight, Jones Day, Kutak Rock, Morrison and Foerster, Skadden Arps, and Vinson & Elkins, to name a few, have hundreds of attorneys spread nationally and internationally.[1] Their clients, while referred to as firm clients, are often represented through a single office independent of other offices of the firm. Firms make lateral hires on a regular basis at their many different offices both within and outside of the United States. Mergers also have become a regular feature whereby smaller firms and specialized practices are being absorbed by bigger firms.[2] There is as well increasing mobility in the

**1.** All these firms have offices in at least 10 major U.S. cities and some of them like Jones Day, Holland and Knight, Baker and McKenzie also have international offices.

**2.** NLJ 250: *The Losers Are Often the Winners*, http://www.law.com/special/professionals/nlj250/nlj250_2000_fin.html (Nov. 29, 2000) (more mergers predicted on the basis that big firms grew at a rate of 14% while smaller firms grew by only 2.5% for the year 1999–2000). Moreover, on occasion,

practice. Attorneys not only are moving from one firm to another but also from government service to private firm practice and vice versa. A major recurrent dilemma is conflicts of interest.

Conflicts may occur with respect to current as well as former clients. A simultaneous representation (current client) conflict arises where an attorney or a law firm represents a client with an interest directly adverse to an existing client. One scenario implicating concern in this context is when one office of a mega-firm procures a client whose interests are directly adverse to an existing client served through another office of the firm. Such a situation would occur, for example, when an attorney in the Denver office of a firm is approached by a prospective client to represent it in a breach of contract suit against a "blue chip" publicly-held company, represented in securities and corporate matters through that firm's New York City office.[3]

Disqualification on grounds of successive representation is the result when an attorney represents at different times, clients with materially adverse interests in matters that are substantially related. A conflict dilemma in successive representation may arise, for instance, when a firm makes a lateral hire from another law firm or when a former government attorney moves to private practice. It is not uncommon for an attorney in government service, like the FTC, the IRS or the SEC, to join a firm which is involved in a case or related matter in which he/she had participated in some way.[4] Also, attorneys who move from one law firm to another, may find that their "new" firms represent interests that are adverse to their former clients.

large firms merge with one another to create a mega firm. The merger of Locke and Liddell Sapp to form Locke Liddell serves as one example.

**3.** *See* Steinberg & Sharpe, *Attorney Conflicts of Interest: The Need for a Coherent Framework*, 66 Notre Dame L. Rev. 1, 34 (1990).

**4.** *See* Cutler, *Conflicts of Interest*, 30 Emory L.J. 1015, 1025 (1981).

While the personal disqualification of an individual attorney is significant, a more important issue from a law firm's perspective is whether one attorney's disqualification on ethical grounds can be imputed to disqualify the firm as a whole. A key basis for such imputed disqualification is the presumption of shared confidences.[5] Under this principle, "knowledge by any member of a law firm is knowledge by all of the attorneys in the firm, partners as well as associates."[6] It is presumed that a lawyer shares client confidences with his firm colleagues. The presumption is grounded on perceptions regarding the realities of law firm practice: "Clients come and go throughout the firm's offices and documents are processed by many hands and necessarily pass before many eyes. Files and documents lie on secretaries' desks and are centrally accessible in file rooms and duplicating offices; the notes of associates are spread on library tables; computer systems bring information before many different viewers."[7] Therefore, the assumption is that information in a law firm is easily accessible even if it is not purposefully shared by attorneys among themselves. Imputed disqualification is also based on the belief that since a fee from one client generally benefits the entire firm, affiliated lawyers will tend to support violations of ethical obligations by a firm member.[8]

The vicarious disqualification rule thus has been principally adopted to protect (1) loyalty towards clients as well as (2) clients' confidences. The Model Rules, for example, generally provide that if one lawyer of a firm is

**5.** *See Kala v. Aluminum Smelting and Refining Co.*, 688 N.E.2d 258, 265 (Ohio 1998).

**6.** *Adams v. Aerojet–General Corp.*, 86 Cal.App.4th 1324, 1333, 104 Cal.Rptr.2d 116 (Cal. Ct.App.2001).

**7.** C. Wolfram, *Modern Legal Ethics* 391 (1986).

**8.** American Law Institute, *Restatement of the Law Governing Lawyers* § 123 cmt. (b) (2000). *See also*, G. Hazard & W. Hodes, 1 *The Law of Lawyering* § 14.3, at 14–6, (3d ed. 2001).

disqualified from representing a client, no other lawyer of that firm can knowingly represent that client[9] unless the client consents.[10] The American Law Institute's (ALI) Restatement of the Law Governing Lawyers takes a similar approach, providing that personal disqualification of a lawyer on conflicts grounds is imputed to lawyers affiliated with the disqualified attorney.[11]

A purported mechanism used to avoid firm disqualification is to "screen" the disqualified attorney so that no information can be exchanged between that attorney and other lawyers of the firm. This device is also referred to as the "Chinese wall" or "ethical wall." A screen or a wall is a "fictional device" used to prevent firm-wide disqualification when: (1) a member of the firm, while at a different firm (or government agency), represented a party who is an adversary of a client represented by her new firm in a substantially related matter;[12] or (2) a lawyer of the firm represents an interest adversarial to an existing client. The usual ways of implementing screening are "restricting a member's access to files, informing attorneys working on the case of the barrier, and excluding the disqualified member

**9.** Model Rules of Prof. Conduct, Rule 1.10(a).

**10.** *Id.* Rule 1.10(c). *See also*, ABA Comm. on Ethics and Professional Responsibility, Formal Opinion 88–356 (1988) (permitting screening mechanisms to insulate "temporary" attorneys, thereby averting firm-wide disqualification).

**11.** *Restatement of the Law Governing Lawyers* § 123. *See generally* N. Crystal, *Professional Responsibility–Problems of Practice and the Profession* 221–232 (1990); S. Gillers, *Regulation of Lawyers* 362–389 (6th ed. 2002); G. Hazard, S. Koniak & R. Cramton, *The Law and Ethics of Lawyering* 667–707 (3d ed 1999); T. Morgan & R. Rotunda, *Professional Responsibility–Problems and Materials* 237–266 (7th ed. 2000); J. Noonan & R. Painter, *Professional and Personal Responsibility of the Lawyer* 276–297 (2d ed. 2001); D. Rhode & D. Luban, *Legal Ethics* 501–517 (3d ed. 2001); J. Sutton & J. Dzienkowski, *Professional Responsibility of Lawyers* 233–258 (2d ed. 2002); R. Zitrin & C. Langford, *Legal Ethics in the Practice of Law* 244–254 (2d ed. 2001).

**12.** Wozniak, *Disqualification of Member of Law Firm as Requiring Disqualification of Entire Firm–State Cases*, 6 A.L.R. 5th 242, § 2 (1992).

from fees generated by the representation."[13] The objective is to isolate the attorney who possesses the confidential information from all other affiliated attorneys. Some means of achieving this objective are keeping files under lock and key, color coding the pertinent files with the name of the walled attorney so that anyone allowed access is reminded of the screen, physically separating the office of the disqualified attorney from other attorneys dealing with the matter, and the use of code names for the project. [14]

In conflict dilemmas involving simultaneous representation, courts regard representation of adverse interests by the same firm in the same litigation as "patently improper."[15] Moreover, simultaneous representation of clients having directly adverse interests even with respect to unrelated matters, without client consent, generally is not acceptable.[16] As stated by one court, "[a] serious effect on the attorney-client relationship may follow if the client discovers from a source other than the attorney that he is being sued in a different matter by the attorney."[17] In such circumstances, the existing client's consent after full disclosure by the subject attorney is required to avoid disqualification.[18] The Model Rules allow such representation only if each client "gives informed consent, confirmed in writing," and the attorney reasonably believes that he/she "will be able to provide competent and diligent representation to each affected client."[19]

But, will disqualification of a particular attorney be imputed to other attorneys, including other offices of the firm situated in different locales which never had

**13.** *Id.*

**14.** R. Simon, *Simon's New York Code of Professional Responsibility Annotated*, DR 5–105, at 347 (2000).

**15.** *See, e.g., People ex rel. Department of Corps. v. SpeeDee Oil Change Sys., Inc.*, 86 Cal. Rptr.2d 816, 819 (Cal.1999).

**16.** *See* G. Hazard & W. Hodes, *supra* note 8, § 11.4, at 11–7.

**17.** *IBM v. Levin*, 579 F.2d 271, 280 (3d Cir. 1978).

**18.** *Id.*

**19.** Model Rules of Prof. Conduct, Rules 1.7(b)(2), (b)(4), 1.10(c).

any contact with the firm's client? The same traditional doctrine of firm-wide imputation has been applied irrespective of firm size or "geographical scope" of counsel.[20] This is because the rule against simultaneous adverse representation is primarily based on the principle of undivided loyalty of an attorney towards her client. Undivided loyalty helps foster "public confidence in the legal profession and the judicial process."[21] Many clients tend to identify legal representation not by the particular attorneys, but by the firm. Therefore, the duty of loyalty is extended to encompass both the lawyer and her firm. For many courts, the appearance of impropriety is also a key concern.[22] It appears improper if an attorney in the firm is representing an existing client's adversary, even if the matter is unrelated. Therefore, none of the attorneys in the firm, even if they had no contact with the existing client and are in a different locale, can represent interests directly adverse to that client even in matters unrelated to the area of representation.

Courts also reason that an adversarial posture towards an existing client may impact the "independent judgment" of the lawyer towards that client.[23] A lawyer may be influenced by a client's importance (such as a blue-chip publicly held company that generates lucrative revenues for the firm) and thereby advance its interests at the cost of the smaller client.[24] Further, the breach of the lawyer's duty of loyalty may have adverse effects on the United States' legal system in which "opposing attorneys, within the bounds of legal and ethical norms, will engage in a zealous, uninhibited presentation of their client's position."[25] Divided loyalties "impair a

**20.** *Westinghouse Electric Corp. v. Kerr–McGee Corp.*, 580 F.2d 1311, 1312, 1318 (7th Cir. 1978).

**21.** *People ex rel. Department of Corps. v. SpeeDee Oil Change Sys., Inc.*, 86 Cal. Rptr.2d 816, 824 (Cal. 1999).

**22.** *Levin*, 579 F.2d at 283.

**23.** *Id.* at 280.

**24.** C. Wolfram, *supra* note 7, at 349.

**25.** Steinberg & Sharpe, *supra* note 3, 66 Notre Dame L. Rev. at 33.

lawyer's representation'' and adversely impact the adversarial nature of the system.[26] In view of the foregoing principles, courts generally have not thus far permitted screening to avert firm-wide disqualification in simultaneous representation cases.[27] However, a client's informed consent based on adequate disclosure frequently will eliminate the conflict dilemma in cases of simultaneous adverse representation.[28]

With respect to successive representation situations, attorney loyalty and protecting clients' confidences are key concerns.[29] The relationship between an attorney and his client is premised on the duty of undivided loyalty and confidentiality towards a client.[30] These duties continue even after representation has been completed and regardless whether an attorney moves to a new firm.[31]

Duties toward a former client are underscored by the Model Rules. These rules prohibit, absent client consent, a lawyer who represented a former client in a matter from subsequently representing another person "in the same or a substantially related matter in which that person's interests are materially adverse to the interests of the former client.''[32] Even if the lawyer

**26.** *Id.*

**27.** *See, e.g., Westinghouse Electric Corp. v. Kerr–McGee Corp.*, 580 F.2d 1311, 1321 (7th Cir.1978); *In re Cendant Corp. Securities Litigation*, 124 F.Supp.2d 235, 247 (D.N.J. 2000).

**28.** C. Wolfram, *supra* note 7, at 352. The issue of client "informed consent" is discussed in Scenario VI. *See generally* Painter, *Advance Waiver of Conflicts*, 13 Geo. J. Leg. Eth. 289 (2000); Zacharias, *Waiving Conflicts of Interest*, 108 Yale L.J. 407 (1998).

**29.** *Kassis v. Teacher's Ins. & Annuity Ass'n*, 93 N.Y.2d 611, 616, 717 N.E.2d 674 (N.Y.1999).

**30.** Beck, *Legal Malpractice in Texas*, 50 Baylor L. Rev. 605, 608 (1998).

**31.** *See People ex rel. Department of Corps. v. SpeeDee Oil Change Sys. Inc.*, 86 Cal.Rptr.2d 816, 825 (Cal.1999).

**32.** Model Rules of Prof. Conduct, Rule 1.9(a). *See id.* Rules 1.9(b), (c), 1.10. *See generally* Aronson, *Conflict of Interest*, 52 Wash. L. Rev. 807 (1977); Wolfram, *Former Client Conflicts*, 10 Geo. J. Leg. Eth. 677 (1997); *Developments in the Law—Conflicts of Interest in the Legal Profession,* 94 Harv. L. Rev. 1244 (1981).

herself did not personally represent the subject client but her former firm had, upon moving to a new firm, she cannot represent a new client materially adverse to the interests of the former firm's client in the same or a substantially related matter if she had acquired confidential information about that client "that is material to the matter."[33] However, if the lawyer's participation was of a "peripheral nature," a number of courts allow the lawyer to rebut the presumption that she had acquired "material" confidential information.[34] With respect to whether the suspect attorney possesses confidential information, it will be sufficient if the attorney simply had the opportunity (in terms of her involvement with the representation) to acquire information pertinent to the current representation.[35] Such cases will be fact-intensive. But generally, if the lawyer's participation involved discovery, conferences with the client and the like, she will be deemed to have received confidential information.[36]

As in simultaneous adverse representation, in cases of successive representation, disqualification of one lawyer has traditionally led to disqualification of the entire firm.[37] Vicarious disqualification in subsequent representation therefore "protects client confidences from misuse in substantially related and adverse litigation, frees the former client from any anxiety that matters disclosed to an attorney will subsequently be used against it in related litigation and provides a clear and readily administered test encouraging self-enforcement among members of the legal profession."[38]

**33.** Model Rule 1.9(b).

**34.** *See, e.g., Silver Chrysler Plymouth, Inc. v. Chrysler Motors Corp.*, 518 F.2d 751, 756–757 (2d Cir.1975).

**35.** *See* G. Hazard & W. Hodes, *supra* note 8, § 13.5, at 13–13. *See also, Schwed v. General Elec. Co.*, 990 F.Supp. 113, 116 (N.D.N.Y.1998).

**36.** *See generally Kassis*, 93 N.Y.2d 611, 717 N.E.2d 674 (N.Y.1999); *Schwed*, 990 F.Supp. 113 (N.D.N.Y.1998).

**37.** *See, e.g., Flatt v. Superior Ct.*, 36 Cal.Rptr.2d 537, 541 (Cal.1994).

**38.** *Kassis*, 93 N.Y. 2d at 616.

Like simultaneous representation, there is a presumption that confidences are shared among lawyers (and other personnel such as paralegals) of a law firm. The methodology in successive representation matters involves a two-step process. In general, before considering a motion of firm-wide imputed disqualification, courts first determine whether the circumstances require disqualification of the individual attorney. Personal disqualification is based on the scope of the attorney's activities in the prior representation as well as application of the "substantial relationship" test.[39]

The "substantial relationship" test seeks to determine the similarities in the issues and contexts implicated with respect to the current and the former representations. The standard historically has been defined as follows:

> "[T]he former client need show no more than that the matters embraced within the pending suit wherein his former attorney appears on behalf of his adversary are substantially related to the matters or cause of action wherein the attorney previously represented him, the former client. The Court will assume that during the course of the former representation confidences were disclosed to the attorney bearing on the subject matter of the representation. It will not inquire into their nature and extent."[40]

Only after the attorney is determined to be disqualified, does the question of her law firm's disqualification arise. Traditionally, disqualification of the attorney on grounds of "substantial relationship" results in automatic disqualification of the firm.[41] However, a number of courts have reformulated the rigid test of "substan-

**39.** *See* Hagan & Kaufman, *The Chinese Wall: A Limited Remedy for Conflicts of Interest,* C641, ALI–ABA 187, 217–218 (1991).

**40.** *T.C. Theatre Corp. v. Warner Bros. Pictures,* 113 F.Supp. 265, 268 (E.D.N.Y. 1953).

**41.** *See In re Marriage of Zimmerman,* 16 Cal.App.4th 556, 563, 20 Cal.Rptr.2d 132 (Cal.Ct.App.1993).

tial relationship'' and allow counsel to rebut the presumption by showing that the attorney was not in a position to have obtained confidential information.[42] For example, if the lawyer had performed only routine and peripheral functions (such as conducting solely legal research) and could not have acquired confidential information, neither the individual attorney nor the law firm will be disqualified.[43]

But if the ''substantial relationship'' test is satisfied and the attorney is determined to have had access to confidential information based on the nature of his involvement in the prior case, the traditional view is that the law firm will be disqualified. This presumption of shared confidences is usually regarded as irrebuttable.[44] Indeed, this irrebuttable presumption may be extended by some courts to paralegals and secretaries.[45] However, a change is being noticed in some jurisdictions given the nature of law practice today.

The Model Rules do not permit screening to avert firm-wide disqualification when a personally disqualified private attorney moves from one firm to another.[46] On the other hand, the ALI Restatement of the Law Governing Lawyers permits screening of private attorneys if timely and adequate notice is provided to all subject clients (former as well as current) and the confidential information possessed by the subject attorney is unlikely

**42.** G. Hazard & W. Hodes, *supra* note 8, § 14.9, at 14–24. *See also, Nissan Motor Corp. v. Orozco*, 595 So.2d 240 (Fla.Dist. Ct.App.1992); *In re Marriage of Zimmerman,* 16 Cal.App.4th 556, 20 Cal.Rptr.2d 132 (Cal.Ct. App.1993) (although the court determined that the former and current representations were substantially similar, it held that disqualification was not warranted where the contact of the attorney was ''brief and insubstantial'').

**43.** *See Nissan Motor Corp.*, 595 So. 2d at 243.

**44.** *See, e.g., State v. Ehlers*, 631 N.W.2d 471, 482 (Neb. 2001).

**45.** *Cf. In re American Home Products Corp.*, 985 S.W.2d 68, 74 (Tex.1998), *citing, Phoenix Founders, Inc. v. Marshall*, 887 S.W.2d 831, 834 (Tex.1994).

**46.** Model Rules of Prof. Conduct, Rule 1.10.

to be important in the subsequent matter.[47]

Many of the state ethical codes are consistent with the Model Rules. These state ethical codes deem the sharing of confidences among law firm attorneys as an irrebuttable presumption, which cannot be overridden by screening when a private lawyer is concerned.[48] New York, for example, does not permit a law firm, absent informed client consent, to escape imputed disqualification.[49] In New York, even a well-constructed screening mechanism is not enough to avoid law firm disqualification if a former client objects and the personally disqualified attorney has the opportunity to possess the former client's confidences.[50] According to one authority, "as of now, it will be a rare case where a court will deny a motion to disqualify a law firm simply because the firm has established a screen around a personally disqualified attorney—and small firms stand virtually no chance because the lawyers in small firms tend to be collegial, frequently discussing their cases with each other and sharing confidential information and strategy."[51]

Some courts that reject screening as rebutting the presumption of shared confidences believe that public suspicion of the legal profession outweighs the interest

**47.** *Restatement of the Law Governing Lawyers* § 124(2).

**48.** *See, e.g., Roberts v. Hutchins*, 572 So.2d 1231 (Ala. 1990) (under local rules of professional conduct, screening not available to attorneys moving between private law firms). *Accord, Edward J. De Bartolo Corp. v. Petrin*, 516 So.2d 6 (Fla. Dist.Ct.App.1987); *Weglarz v. Bruck*, 470 N.E.2d 21 (Ill.App. Ct.1984); *Monroe v. City of Topeka*, 988 P.2d 228 (Kan. 1999); *State ex rel. Freezer Services, Inc. v. Mullen*, 458 N.W.2d 245 (Neb.1990); *Kassis v. Teacher's Ins. & Annuity Ass'n*, 93 N.Y.2d 611, 717 N.E.2d 674 (N.Y.1999); *Petroleum Wholesale, Inc. v. Marshall*, 751 S.W.2d 295, 300 (Tex.App.1988).

**49.** R. Simon, *supra* note 14, DR 5–108, at 377. *See Kassis v. Teacher's Ins. & Annuity Ass'n*, 93 N.Y.2d 611, 717 N.E.2d 674 (N.Y.1999) (stating, however, that screening mechanism should be set up when the attorney possesses no material confidential information to remove even the appearance of impropriety).

**50.** *See* R. Simon, *supra* note 14, DR 5–108, at 377, *citing, Kassis*, 93 N.Y.2d 611, 717 N.E.2d 674 (N.Y.1999).

**51.** R. Simon, *supra* note 14, DR 5–105, at 347.

of a party in obtaining the counsel of his choice.[52] These courts reason that when the case involves a private attorney with actual knowledge of a former client's confidences, "such an appearance of impropriety arises that not even an effective Chinese wall can allay public suspicion."[53]

Irrespective that a majority of state ethical codes and courts currently do not allow screening in the private attorney setting, the situation is changing. For two decades, a number of federal courts have allowed counsel to rebut this presumption.[54] The modern day practice of law has led to the growing belief that a non-rebuttable presumption in the successive representation context is "out of touch" with reality.[55] Attorneys no longer stay with one firm throughout their entire careers. In such a mobile practice, automatic disqualification would cast immense hardship on "the lawyer, the firm and the firm's clients."[56] Costs associated with disqualification are also formidable. Not only does the firm lose a prospective client but the client too has to bear the expense of finding alternate counsel.[57] Automatic disqualification is also disfavored because it makes law firms hesitant to hire lawyers trying to move to other firms.[58] These lawyers "would find themselves cast adrift as 'Typhoid Marys' and clients would find their choice of counsel substantially diminished."[59] Further, a strict rule favoring vicarious disqualification leads to abuse as it is often used as a litigation tactic seeking to

**52.** *See, e.g., Petroleum Wholesale, Inc. v. Marshall*, 751 S.W.2d 295, 300–301 (Tex.App. 1988).

**53.** *Id.* at 300.

**54.** *See, e.g., Manning v. Waring, Cox, James, Sklar & Allen*, 849 F.2d 222, 225 (6th Cir.1988); *Schiessle v. Stephens*, 717 F.2d 417, 421 (7th Cir. 1983).

**55.** *Adams v. Aerojet Gen. Corp.*, 86 Cal.App.4th 1324, 1336, 104 Cal.Rptr.2d 116 (Cal. Ct.App.2001).

**56.** *In re County of Los Angeles*, 223 F.3d 990, 996 (9th Cir.2000).

**57.** *Adams v. Aerojet Gen. Corp.*, 86 Cal. App. 4th at 1339.

**58.** *In re County of Los Angeles*, 223 F.3d at 996.

**59.** *Id.*

deny an opposing party its counsel of choice.[60]

Further, it may be asserted that the growth of the "mega-firm" has undermined the presumption of shared confidences.[61] Confidences and information are more likely to be shared in a small firm rather than lawyers practicing in different cities in a mega-firm.[62] Due to such changing realities of law practice, a change in the direction of the courts is being noticed. As the Ohio Supreme Court reasoned, "[u]ltimately, one must have faith in the integrity of members of the legal profession to honor their professional oath to uphold the Code of Professional Responsibility, safeguarded by the precautions required to rebut the presumption of shared confidences."[63]

The factors that courts have considered in determining the efficacy of a screening quarantine are: "(1) the size of the firm;[64] (2) the extent of departmentalization within the firm; (3) prohibitions against discussion of the action with the new member; and (4) exclusion of the new member from the relevant files, participation in the action, and sharing in firm earnings from the action."[65] Further, the wall must be timely built and effectively implemented.[66] "To be timely, the wall must be constructed as soon as the potential for conflict

**60.** *See Manning v. Waring, Cox, James, Sklar & Allen*, 849 F.2d 222, 224 (6th Cir.1988) ("Unquestionably, the ability to deny one's opponent the services of capable counsel is a potent weapon.").

**61.** *See* Steinberg & Sharpe, *supra* note 3, 66 Notre Dame L. Rev. at 13.

**62.** *Id.* ("It is quite different to irrebuttably presume that a lawyer in the Chicago office of a 500–lawyer firm obtained confidential information about a client represented by a lawyer in the firm's New York Office.").

**63.** *Kala v. Aluminum Smelting and Refining Co.*, 688 N.E.2d 258, 265 (Ohio 1998). *See also, Clinard v. Blackwood*, 46 S.W.3d 177 (Tenn.2001).

**64.** *Solow v. W.R. Grace & Co.*, 83 N.Y.2d 303, 313, 632 N.E.2d 437 (N.Y. 1994) ("In firms characterized by informality, disqualification will be imposed as a matter of law without a hearing.").

**65.** *Petroleum Wholesale, Inc. v. Marshall*, 751 S.W.2d 295, 297 (Tex.App.1988).

**66.** *See* Hagan & Kaufman, *supra* note 39, at 223.

exists.''[67] But under certain circumstances, an ethical wall cannot provide an effective screen, no matter how timely and well constructed it is. This happens particularly when the size of the firm is so small that an effective screen cannot practically be implemented.[68]

The current situation in California highlights the uncertainty in this context. California ethical rules at this time do not address either imputed disqualification or the use of screening to avert vicarious disqualification in the private law firm context.[69] But as viewed by a number of California courts, ''[n]o amount of assurances or screening procedures, no 'cone of silence,' could ever convince the opposing party that the confidences would not be used to its disadvantage.''[70] Hence, although vicarious disqualification is decided in California on a case-by-case basis, the state appellate courts generally have ruled that firm-wide imputation is automatic.[71] In fact, they have extended the presumption to include summer associates.[72]

However, a change appears to be occurring in California. While the California Supreme Court has not specifically addressed the question as to whether the

**67.** *Id. See LaSalle National Bank v. County of Lake*, 703 F.2d 252, 259 (7th Cir.1983) (a wall built months after conflict became apparent does not rebut the presumption).

**68.** *See Cheng v. GAF Corp.*, 631 F.2d 1052, 1058 (2d Cir. 1980) (the firm was too small for a screening mechanism to be effective); R. Simon, *supra* note 14, at 377.

**69.** *See* Gibbons–White, *Migratory Lawyers in Private Practice: Should California Approve the Use of Ethical Walls?*, 33 Loy. L.A. L. Rev. 161, 163 (1999).

**70.** *Adams v. Aerojet–Gen. Corp.*, 86 Cal.App.4th 1324, 1334, 104 Cal.Rptr.2d 116 (Cal. Ct.App.2001), *quoting*, *Cho v. Superior Court*, 39 Cal.App.4th 113, 125, 45 Cal.Rptr.2d 863 (Cal.Ct.App.1995).

**71.** *See* Gibbons–White, *supra* note 69, 33 Loy. L.A. L. Rev. at 163.

**72.** *Id.*, *citing*, *Actel Corp. v. Quicklogic Corp.*, 1996 WL 297045 (N.D.Cal.1996). Generally, screening of nonlawyers is more readily permitted by the courts provided the screen is implemented promptly and effectively. For a discussion of disqualification of paralegals and other nonlawyers, see G. Hazard & W. Hodes, *supra* note 8, § 14.11, at 14–28.

presumption of shared confidences is rebuttable, it implied that "discrete, successive conflicting representations in substantially related matters" may pose less of a threat to the attorney-client relationship.[73] Focussing on this language, the U.S. Court of Appeals for the Ninth Circuit has predicted that California law might change in the near future.[74] According to the Ninth Circuit's interpretation, the California Supreme Court might allow screening to avoid vicarious disqualification of law firms. Ruling to permit screening, the court stated "[i]n resolving this case, we take our cue from the California Supreme Court's recent indication that it may be inclined to follow the path taken by other federal courts."[75] Therefore, although intermediate appellate case law in California still exists that screening is not permitted, the California Supreme Court (as interpreted by the Ninth Circuit) has indicated that a change might be forthcoming.

Hence, federal courts generally have been more permissive about screening than state courts.[76] A number of federal courts have held that if a screen is timely and effectively implemented, it can rebut the presumption of shared confidences in successive representation matters.[77] These courts recognize that firm-wide automatic disqualification is a drastic measure and should be imposed only when circumstances indicate that no feasible alternative exists for protecting client confidences.[78]

**73.** *People ex rel. Dep't of Corps. v. Speedee Oil Change Sys., Inc.*, 86 Cal.Rptr.2d 816, 828, 980 P.2d 371 (Cal.1999).

**74.** *In re County of Los Angeles*, 223 F.3d 990, 995 (9th Cir.2000).

**75.** *Id.* at 997.

**76.** See, e.g., *In re County of Los Angeles*, 223 F.3d 990 (9th Cir.2000); *Manning v. Waring, Cox, James, Sklar & Allen*, 849 F.2d 222 (6th Cir.1988); *Schiessle v. Stephens*, 717 F.2d 417, 421 (7th Cir.1983).

**77.** *See, e.g., In re County of Los Angeles*, 223 F.3d at 996.

**78.** *See Schiessle v. Stephens*, 717 F.2d at 420, *quoting*, *Freeman v. Chicago Musical Instrument Co.*, 689 F.2d 715, 721 (7th Cir.1982). *See generally* Bateman, *Return to the Ethics As a Standard for Attorney Disqualification*, 33 Duquesne L. Rev. 249 (1995); Penegar, *The Loss of Innocence: A Brief Histo-*

Therefore, institutional screening mechanisms can be implemented to effectively insulate the disqualified attorney from the rest of the firm.

Moreover, when the conflict of interest dilemma concerns a former government attorney, the courts and ethical rules are more flexible. In the case of a personally disqualified government attorney who has moved to private practice, disqualification of the firm can be avoided by timely and effectively screening the particular lawyer.[79] The personally disqualified lawyer must not receive any part of the fee from the client and written notice must be provided to the appropriate government agency.[80] The rationale is that if strict firm-wide disqualification were to be applied to former government lawyers, "the potential effect on the government would be unduly burdensome."[81] Since the government's sphere of representation involves all private citizens and organizations, disallowing screening, proponents claim, will adversely impact the government's efforts to attract adept attorneys to government service.[82] Automatic firm-wide vicarious disqualification thus would cause qualified attorneys not to seek government jobs due to fear that government service would cause them to be shunned by prospective private employers.

The following Scenario illustrates a common dilemma faced by attorneys and law firms in these times of lawyer mobility and mega firms.

*ry of Law Firm Disqualification in the Courts*, 8 Geo. J. Leg. Eth. 831 (1995); Reich, Vernick & Horn, *Screening Mechanisms: A Broader Application?*, 72 Temple L. Rev. 1023 (1999); Rotunda, *Conflicts Problems When Representing Members of Corporate Families*, 72 Notre Dame L. Rev. 655 (1997).

**79.** *See* Model Rules of Prof. Conduct, Rule 1.11.

**80.** *Id.*

**81.** *Id.* Rule 1.10 cmt. 5.

**82.** *See, e.g.*, *Armstrong v. McAlpin*, 625 F.2d 433, 443 (2d Cir.1980) (en banc). *See generally* Morgan, *Appropriate Limits on Participation by a Former Agency Official in Matters Before an Agency*, 1980 Duke L.J. 14 (1980); Mundheim, *Conflict of Interest and the Former Government Employee: Rethinking the Revolving Door*, 14 Creighton L. Rev. 707 (1981).

## SCENARIO

Alexandra Franco graduated from the University of Missouri–Columbia School of Law in 2001.[83] After graduation, she joined the St. Louis law firm of Delaney Gibbs & Showater, L.L.C. as an Associate in the firm's real estate section. In the Spring of 2002, Franco worked on the sale of real estate—a shopping center—from her firm's client Fendum Associates L.P. to Luger Properties, Inc. As the junior lawyer on the transaction, Franco conducted legal research, wrote a legal memorandum on a zoning-related issue to the firm's partner (Teresa Fielding) working on the transaction, drafted some of the minor closing documents, and met with the two general partners of Fendum Associates L.P. on one twenty minute occasion when Fielding was also present. The transaction timely closed without undue complication.

One year later, Franco elects to leave Delaney Gibbs & Showater to join another St. Louis law firm, Olendar & Shawnessey, P.C., as an Associate. A $12,000 signing bonus, $10,000 increase in annual salary and the opportunity to have more "hands-on" experience are the key inducements. After joining Olendar & Shawnessey, Franco learns that the firm's client Luger Properties, Inc., has sued Fendum Associates L.P. in Missouri state court alleging breach of contract, misrepresentation, and fraud in the real estate shopping center transaction that Franco had worked on while at Delaney Gibbs & Showater.

Upon discovering Franco's prior representation of Fendum Associates L.P., Olendar & Shawnessey promptly "screens" her from all contact with the subject litigation. Instructions are sent to all attorneys and employees of the firm that absolutely no communication, written or oral, should be made to Franco regarding this matter. Franco's office located in the firm's real

**83.** Of course, the narrative as set forth in this Scenario, like the other Scenarios in this text, is fictitious.

estate section is in the same building, three floors above the litigation section's offices.

Shortly thereafter, Delaney Gibbs & Showater, on behalf of its client Fendum Associates L.P., files a motion to disqualify the Olendar & Shawnessey firm in the subject litigation. Should the law firm be disqualified under applicable ethical standards? What are the policies implicated?

Should there be a different result if Franco's prior employment had been with a government agency? Suppose, for example, that prior to being an Associate at Delaney Gibbs & Showater, Franco was a staff attorney in the Missouri Attorney General's Department. She participated actively in a staff investigation that focused on suspicious real estate dealings by Fendum Associates L.P. After the investigation was completed, Franco joins Delaney Gibbs & Showater as an Associate. Six months later, the State of Missouri institutes an action alleging fraud against Fendum Associates L.P. Assuming that Franco is effectively and promptly "screened," should Delaney Gibbs & Showater be disqualified from representing Fendum Associates L.P. in this litigation?

# Scenario VIII

## LAWYERS TAKING EQUITY INTERESTS IN THEIR CLIENTS

Although far less common than during the "high-tech" boom, corporate attorneys may accept equity interests in their clients, in addition to or in lieu of cash compensation.[1] These arrangements appear to create conflicts of interest and implicate significant professional and ethical issues. An attorney's personal stake in a client could potentially cloud that attorney's professional and independent judgment. Rather than objectively counseling what is best for that particular client, the attorney could become influenced by what is best for his/her own pocketbook. The American Bar Association (ABA) has opined that while such fee arrangements are not per se unethical, they do constitute business transactions, and must therefore meet certain standards.[2] Among these governing standards are Rules 1.5,[3]

1. *See* Klein, *No Fool For A Client: The Finance and Incentives Behind Stock–Based Compensation For Corporate Attorneys*, 1999 Colum. Bus. L. Rev. 329 (1999); McAlpine, *Getting a Piece of the Action: Should Lawyers Be Allowed to Invest in Their Clients' Stock?*, 47 UCLA L. Rev. 549 (1999); Puri, *Taking Stock of Taking Stock*, 87 Cornell L. Rev. 99 (2001).

2. *See* Model Rule. 1.8 cmt. 1; American Bar Association, *Acquiring Ownership In A Client In Connection With Legal Services*, ABA Formal Op. 00–418 (2000).

3. Model Rule 1.5(a) provides:

1.7,[4] and 1.8[5] of the Model Rules of Professional Conduct.

"A lawyer shall not make an agreement for, charge, or collect an unreasonable fee or an unreasonable amount for expenses. The factors to be considered in determining the reasonableness of a fee include the following:

(1) the time and labor required, the novelty and difficulty of the question involved, and the skill requisite to perform the legal service properly;

(2) the likelihood, if apparent to the client, that the acceptance of the particular employment will preclude other employment by the lawyer;

(3) the fee customarily charged in the locality for similar legal services;

(4) the amount involved and the results obtained;

(5) the time limitations imposed by the client or by the circumstances;

(6) the nature and length of the professional relationship with the client;

(7) the experience, reputation, and ability of the lawyer or lawyers performing the services; and

(8) whether the fee is fixed or contingent."

**4.** Model Rule 1.7 (Conflict of Interest: Current Clients) generally precludes an attorney from representing a client if such representation implicates "a concurrent conflict of interest." A client may waive the conflict if such client "gives informed consent, confirmed in writing," and the attorney reasonably believes that "competent and diligent representation" can be rendered to such client. Rule 1.7 is set forth in Scenario VI *supra* notes 4–6 and accompanying text.

**5.** Model Rule 1.8(a) provides:

"(a) A lawyer shall not enter into a business transaction with a client or knowingly acquire an ownership, possessory, security or other pecuniary interest adverse to a client unless:

(1) the transaction and terms on which the lawyer acquires the interest are fair and reasonable to the client and are fully disclosed and transmitted in writing in a manner that can be reasonably understood by the client;

(2) the client is advised in writing of the desirability of seeking and is given a reasonable opportunity to seek the advice of independent legal counsel on the transaction; and

(3) the client gives informed consent, in a writing signed by the client, to the essential terms of the transaction and the lawyer's role in the transaction, including whether the lawyer is representing the client in the transaction."

Rule 1.5 essentially provides that an attorney's fees must be reasonable.[6] In a traditional fee arrangement, reasonableness can be generally assessed by comparing the overall compensation received by the attorney to the total number of hours billed and the complexity of the issues involved. In an equity compensation structure, however, reasonableness becomes more elusive. First, one must decide at what point reasonableness is to be ascertained. This determination is complicated by the fact that in an equity compensation arrangement the lawyer and client agree upon an amount that may fluctuate significantly after the agreement is executed. Subsequent fluctuations in the value of the company in which the attorney owns an equity interest can significantly impact this compensation amount. Thus, what appears to be reasonable compensation at first, suddenly may seem outrageous a short time later.[7]

For example, a law firm agrees to represent a corporate client as general outside counsel for a one-year period in exchange for a 5% equity interest in the corporation. As of the date of the agreement, this 5% equates to 1000 shares of the corporation's outstanding stock that is valued at $50 per share, resulting in contemplated compensation of $50,000. Ten months later the Company "goes public," having its initial public offering (IPO), at a price of $15 per share. Consequently, the law firm's compensation, which was originally $50,000, is now only $15,000. Or, in the converse, assume the Company has a ten to one stock split and its IPO is priced at $20 per share. The law firm's compen-

**6.** *See* Model Rule 1.5(a), note 3 *supra*.

**7.** *See* G. Hazard & W. Hodes, *The Law of Lawyering* § 12.5 (3d ed. 2001); Klein, *supra* note 1, 1999 Colum. Bus. L. Rev. at 335–337; McAlpine, *supra* note 1, 47 UCLA L. Rev. at 587. *See also*, ABA Formal Opinion No. 00–418, *supra* note 2, at n. 14 (citing Utah Ethics Advisory Committee Opinion 98–13, 1998 WL 863904 (1998) for the principle that "in addition to factors enumerated in [Model] Rule 1.5(a), the lawyer also should consider in determining the reasonableness of a fee when accepting client stock: (i) the liquidity of the stock, (ii) whether and when it can be expected to be publicly traded, (iii) any restrictions on its transfer, and (iv) its presently anticipated value....").

sation is now $200,000, (10,000 shares at $20 per share) or $150,000 more than the amount initially agreed upon between the law firm and the client.

These situations demonstrate some potential obstacles to the traditional determinations of reasonableness with respect to attorneys' fees. Model Rule 1.5 provides little guidance when attempting to determine when the reasonableness assessment is to be made.[8] However, ascertaining reasonableness at any time other than when the agreement between the client and attorney is made seems misplaced. Under this view, a review of the lawyer's fee is appropriate only at the time it is agreed upon between the lawyer and the client. In the example above, the agreement contemplated $50,000 in compensation to counsel. Whether that constitutes a reasonable fee should be determined at the time of the agreement. Thus, this approach posits that it is irrelevant for Model Rule 1.5 purposes that the fee may subsequently experience significant fluctuations.[9]

The ABA's opinion on this subject seems to concur, stating: "For purposes of judging the fairness and reasonableness of the transaction and its terms, the Committee's opinion is that when assessing the reasonableness of a contingent fee, only the circumstances reasonably ascertainable at the time of the transaction should be considered."[10] In such a situation, it is counsel's responsibility to disclose to the client in writing the essential terms and reasonably foreseeable consequences of the stock compensation agreement.[11]

**8.** Model Rule 1.5 does list certain factors that are to be taken into consideration in assessing the reasonableness of an attorney's fee. *See* Model Rule 1.5(a), note 3 *supra*. These factors as well as the Comments to Rule 1.5 do not, however, provide any guidance with respect to when the fee reasonableness assessment is to be made.

**9.** *See* Klein, *supra* note 1, 1999 Colum. Bus. Law. Rev. at 336.

**10.** ABA Formal Opinion No. 00–418, note 2 *supra*.

**11.** *Id. See* Model Rule 1.8(a) & cmts. 1–3.

Model Rule 1.7 serves as the general prohibition on lawyers engaging in conflicts of interest within the scope of their client representations. A lawyer with an equity interest in a client could render legal services with less than the requisite independence of judgment with respect to that client, since the lawyer now has a personal interest at stake. According to Rule 1.7(a)(2), the lawyer normally may not represent the client "if there is a significant risk that the representation of [that] client will be materially limited by . . . a personal interest of the lawyer."[12] Nonetheless, even if counsel's representation of a client may be materially limited by such lawyer's personal interest, so long as the attorney "reasonably believes that the lawyer will be able to provide competent and diligent representation to [the] client" and the "client gives informed consent, confirmed in writing," the lawyer may undertake the representation.[13] Thus, the challenging inquiry is: when does the lawyer's ability to represent the client become materially limited by the lawyer's pecuniary ownership (e.g., stock) interest in the client so that, even with informed client consent, the lawyer will be disabled from rendering competent and diligent representation?[14]

**12.** Moreover, Model Rule 1.8 cmt. 3 provides:

> "The risk to the client is greatest . . . when the lawyer's financial interest otherwise poses a significant risk that the lawyer's representation of the client will be materially limited by the lawyer's financial interest in the transaction. Here the lawyer's role requires that the lawyer must comply, not only with the requirements of paragraph (a) [of Rule 1.8], but also with the requirements of Rule 1.7. Under Rule [1.7], the lawyer must disclose the risks associated with the lawyer's dual role as both legal adviser and participant in the transaction, such as the risk that the lawyer will structure the transaction or give legal advice in a way that favors the lawyer's interests at the expense of the client. Moreover, the lawyer must obtain the client's informed consent. In some cases, the lawyer's interest may be such that Rule 1.7 will preclude the lawyer from seeking the client's consent to the transaction."

**13.** *Id.* Model Rule 1.7(a), 1.7(b)(2), (b)(4).

**14.** *See* McAlpine, *supra* note 1, 47 UCLA L. Rev. at 583; Puri, *supra* note 1, 87 Cornell L. Rev. at 140–144.

When responding to this inquiry, counsel must focus on the general conflict of interest provisions in Model Rule 1.7, the reasonableness of attorney fee provisions in Rule 1.5, and the criteria for entering into a business transaction with a client set forth in Rule 1.8(a). The commentary to Rule 1.8 makes clear that equity based (e.g., stock) attorney-client compensation arrangements are business transactions that trigger the requirements of that Rule.[15] Generally, Rule 1.8(a) requires that: first, prior to agreeing to equity based compensation, the lawyer must ensure that the transaction and terms of the arrangement are fair and reasonable to the client, and that they have been fully disclosed in an understandable manner to the client in writing;[16] second, the lawyer must inform the client in writing of the benefits of seeking the advice of independent legal counsel and such client must be provided with a reasonable opportunity to seek such advice;[17] and, third, the client must give informed consent in writing to the essential terms of the agreement as well as to the attorney's role with respect thereto.[18]

The prevalence of equity compensation during the 1990s was largely a result of the rise in start-up companies dominating the high-tech sector.[19] These innovative companies oftentimes do not have the cash on hand to afford quality legal services. What they do offer, however, is the opportunity for a law firm to become an early stage investor. This usually allows the firm (or the individual attorneys) to purchase the company's stock at an attractive price. If and when the company goes public, the law firm theoretically has an unlimited upside potential payoff. On the other hand, because many of these companies "go broke," the law firm also faces

**15.** *See* Model Rule 1.8 cmt. 1; ABA Formal Opinion No. 00–418, note 2 *supra*.

**16.** Model Rule 1.8(a)(1). *See* C. Wolfram, *Modern Legal Ethics* § 8.11 (1986).

**17.** *Id.* Model Rule 1.8(a)(2).

**18.** *Id.* Model Rule 1.8(a)(3).

**19.** *See* McAlpine, *supra* note 1, 47 UCLA L. Rev. at 550–558.

considerable downside exposure.[20]

From the company's perspective, having the law firm take an equity interest provides congruent goal alliance.[21] With the amount of the law firm's fee largely dependent on the success of the company's stock offering, counsel has additional incentive to ensure that the offering is a success. Furthermore, the law firm's financial stake in the company may have a positive signaling effect in the venture capital and institutional investor markets.[22] Presumably, a reputable law firm would not invest in a start-up company unless the company was bound for success. Thus, the law firm's equity investment sends a signal to the marketplace that the company's stock is a good investment.[23] Not surprisingly, if the price of the company's stock subsequently diminishes in value or, even worse, if the company declares bankruptcy, legal counsel who invested in the company's securities may well become targets for disgruntled investors and regulators.

The following Scenario highlights many of the ethical issues that may arise when the client pays its attorneys' fees in company stock rather than cash.

## SCENARIO

Super Hi–Tech, Inc. is a California based technology company that is just getting off the ground. Willard Wendell, the company's founder and CEO, decides that it is time to retain legal counsel to assist the Company in moving forward. Wendell wants a mid to large size law firm that is known not only for its quality reputation, but also for its ability to attract high dollar venture

**20.** *Id.* at 577–582. *See* Klein, *supra* note 1, 1999 Colum. Bus. L. Rev. at 352; Puri, *supra* note 1, 87 Cornell L. Rev. at 114.

**21.** *See* McAlpine *supra* note 1, 47 UCLA L. Rev. at 572; Puri, *supra* note 1, 87 Cornell L. Rev. at 140.

**22.** *See* Klein *supra* note 1, 1999 Colum. Bus. L. Rev. at 346.

**23.** *See* McAlpine, *supra* note 1, 47 UCLA L. Rev. at 572–574; Puri, *supra* note 1, 87 Cornell L. Rev. at 104–106.

capitalists and, eventually, institutional investors. While Super Hi–Tech is currently a privately-held corporation, Wendell has big plans for the future, and dreams of dollar signs after an initial public offering (IPO) of the Company's stock.

Danielle Danford is a third year corporate associate with Connor, Chiu, & Cohen (CCC), a prestigious Los Angeles based law firm. Wendell and Danford went to the same small liberal arts college and, at an alumni function, Danford heard of Wendell's rumored success in the technology industry. As a third year associate, Danford is starting to feel pressure to bring in a few of her own clients.

Shortly thereafter, remembering what she heard about Wendell, Danford decides to contact him. The call could not have come at a better time. Wendell is ready to retain Danford's law firm immediately. The problem is that the retainer for Danford's law firm is $25,000, and Super Hi–Tech has about $12,000 in the bank. After learning more about Super Hi–Tech, Danford becomes enthused about the Company and its conceptual products. She meets with the law firm partner in charge of CCC's Corporate Section, George Henderson, and relays the good news. Not surprisingly, Henderson is less than thrilled about Super Hi–Tech's inability to cover the initial retainer. Danford suggests that in lieu of the retainer, the firm accept as compensation Super Hi–Tech stock. Being envious of some of his acquaintances in other law firms who have made "fortunes" taking stock as fees, Henderson agrees to explore the possibility.

Subsequently, Super Hi–Tech and Connor, Chiu & Cohen agree that CCC will serve as the Company's corporate counsel, will advise it through the process of venture financing, provide contacts to potential investors, and ultimately take the Company public. In return, Super Hi–Tech will compensate the firm $50,000 in stock, up front, and then another $200,000 in stock immediately prior to the initial public offering (IPO).

Super Hi–Tech enjoys huge success. Its products are market blockbusters. The venture capitalists are fighting for a piece of the action, and Wendell, CCC, and the investment bankers realize the time has come to take the Company public. Henderson, Danford, and their team begin the necessary steps, including performing due diligence. Before they are even near completion, however, the market window ripens and analysts predict that this will be the last wave of high-tech IPO success for quite a while. Henderson asks Danford repeatedly why the due diligence is taking so long. Against her better judgment, Danford expedites the process in order to get the deal to market while the market window is still promising. As a result of cursory due diligence, the CCC due diligence team fails to discover a significant "contract" between Super Hi–Tech and one of its customers. The IPO raises over $25 million, and things could not look better. The Company has raised impressive capital, the law firm's investment looks golden, Wendell is a multi-millionaire, and Danford is soon promoted to partner.

Then the technology market heads south, and things begin to unravel. In addition to a sour market, Super Hi–Tech just realized that the product, on which it had pinned much of its future hopes, is a flop. A dejected Wendell calls Danford to discuss the current situation. Wendell wants to know how to inform Super Hi–Tech's shareholders and the investing public of the failed product that the Company has spent the last ten months touting. Normally, CCC advises clients having such a material adverse development to promptly issue a press release.

Before Danford can explain this course of action to Wendell, he tells her that he has some seriously bad news. Danford wonders what could possibly be worse than what she has already heard. Wendell explains that a contract amounting to twelve percent of the Company's revenues, as set forth in the IPO Prospectus, in fact never existed and is "phony." Danford feels her stomach crawl into her throat as she wonders about the contents of her malpractice insurance policy.

Shortly thereafter, you are retained as legal counsel by Connor, Chiu & Cohen to assess the firm's compliance with ethical standards and the risk of liability should lawsuits be brought.

# Scenario IX

# INSIDE COUNSEL

The role of inside counsel[1] has changed dramatically in the last two decades. As Irving Shapiro, former general counsel of DuPont, remarked:

> "In the past, businessmen wore blinders. After hours, they would run to their club, play golf with other businessmen, have a martini—and that was about it.... In a world where government simply took taxes from you and did not interfere with your operations, maybe that idea was sensible. In today's world, it is not."[2]

H.J. Aibel, then chief legal officer of ITT, upon reflecting on the status of inside counsel in the times of yesteryear, commented that "then the generally accepted wisdom [was] that jobs in corporate law departments were for second raters, or lawyers who had failed to make partner at some of the better firms."[3] Today, however, the responsibility and prestige of inside counsel have increased dramatically.[4] Indeed, the issues fac-

**1.** Inside counsel is generally defined as attorneys employed full-time by corporations.

**2.** Loeb, *The Corporate Chiefs' New Class,* Time, Apr. 14, 1980, at 87 (quoting Irving Shapiro).

**3.** Aibel, *Corporate Counsel and Business Ethics: A Personal Review*, 59 Mo. L. Rev. 427, 427 (1994).

**4.** Williams, *The Role of Inside Counsel in Corporate Accountability,* [1979–1980 Transfer Binder] CCH Fed. Sec. L. Rep. ¶ 82,318, at 82,369 (1979). *See* Chayes & Chayes, *Corporate Counsel and the Elite Law Firm,* 37 Stan. L. Rev. 277 (1985);

ing in-house attorneys have become as multifaceted and challenging as those arising in law firms. Inside counsel now plays an active role in shaping corporate events, in assessing corporate policies, and in establishing the tone and standard for corporate conduct.[5] Today, for example, there are legal departments with 400 or more in-house attorneys. Additionally, the American Corporate Counsel Association (ACCA) now numbers more than 10,000 members, and 15% of the American Bar Association members are employed as in-house counsel.[6]

As a full-time employee of his own client, in-house counsel faces the unique situation of being "wedded" to his client. As such, inside counsel is likely to encounter difficult questions of professional independence. For example, when outside counsel has a "difficult" client (such as one that fails to timely pay its bills or one that engages in unethical conduct), the attorney may "walk" from that client.[7] Although the attorney certainly may miss the revenues that the client otherwise would have generated, she normally has the economic leeway to resign from the engagement. However, when inside counsel's client is unduly "difficult" or behaves improperly, counsel must either tolerate such conduct or find another job. Hence, being in-house counsel makes separation and divorce far more onerous.

On the other hand, inside counsel's "marital" relationship to his client has key attributes. One particular-

Daly, *The Cultural, Ethical and Legal Challenges in Lawyering for a Global Organization: The Role of the General Counsel,* 46 Emory L.J. 1057 (1997); Rosen, *The Inside Counsel Movement, Professional Judgment and Organizational Representation,* 64 Ind. L.J. 479 (1989).

**5.** *See* M. Steinberg, *Corporate Internal Affairs: A Corporate and Securities Law Perspective* 251 (1983). *See also,* Williams, note 4 *supra.*

**6.** *See* Frederick, *In Focus: Corporate Counsel Cutting Lawyers May Not Be the Best Way to Cut Costs,* Nat'l L.J., Oct. 17, 1994, at C6.

**7.** *See generally* Model Rules of Prof. Conduct, Rule 1.16 & cmts.; Hemmer, *Resignation of Corporate Counsel: Fulfillment or Abdication of Duty?,* 39 Hastings L.J. 641 (1988).

ly attractive one, for example, is that inside counsel is very much at the center of the key legal functions of the enterprise, including that of corporate law compliance. Moreover, inside counsel in many corporations are involved in business strategy. As a result, she has the financial acumen to understand the benefits and risks of a prospective venture and has the opportunity to communicate with management regarding the economic aspects of a contemplated "deal." In these functions, inside counsel seeks to be perceived within the enterprise as a "can do yes person," while retaining the leverage to effectively say "no" when appropriate.[8]

H.J. Aibel, while discussing his experience as corporate counsel for ITT Corporation, elaborated upon this view:

> "[E]arly involvement of the lawyer often depends upon the prior establishment of a reputation for being a 'team player,' a 'can do lawyer'.... Although it is not easy for inside counsel to bring to the attention of the corporation's Board of Directors situations in which senior management is failing to take appropriate action, in the end, his or her career may depend upon doing so."[9]

As the following discussion illustrates, in-house counsel often confront many challenging issues, such as: (1) client identification and loyalty; (2) the general duty to inquire when offering advice; (3) the obligation to take appropriate action when a corporate fraud or crime is discovered; (4) liability arising under applicable laws; and (5) the implementation of law compliance policies.

The first area of concern facing in-house counsel involves client identification. Stated succinctly, who is

**8.** *See* Creedon, *Lawyer and Executive—The Role of the General Counsel*, 39 Bus. Law. 25 (1983); *How Agile is Your Legal Department?*, Corp. Legal Times, Aug. 1995, at 1, 5 (quoting statements by McDonald's Corp. assistant general counsel Ira S. Feldman that "[a]ll of the lawyers at McDonald's become intimately involved on the business side" and that "lawyer[s] ... wear two hats: a business hat as well as [a] legal hat").

**9.** Aibel, *supra* note 3, 59 Mo. L. Rev. at 431–432.

inside counsel's client? According to both the American Bar Association (ABA) Model Code of Professional Responsibility (Model Code) and the Model Rules of Professional Conduct (Model Rules), the client is the corporate entity. For example, The Model Code provides that:

> "A lawyer employed or retained by a corporation or similar entity owes his allegiance to the entity and not to a stockholder, director, officer, employee, representative, or other person connected with the entity. In advising the entity, a lawyer should keep paramount its interests and his professional judgment should not be influenced by the personal desires of any person or organization."[10]

Similarly, ABA Model Rule 1.13(a) provides that "[a] lawyer employed or retained by an organization represents the organization acting through its duly authorized constituents."[11] The American Law Institute's Restatement of the Law Governing Lawyers likewise states that "the lawyer represents the interests of the organization as defined by its responsible agents acting pursuant to the organization's decision-making procedures."[12]

The seeming simplicity of these rules often breaks down in practice, however, because the organizational entity can "speak" and make decisions only through its "authorized constituents," including such corporation's officers, directors, shareholders, and employees.[13] Due to the close working relationship that develops between in-house counsel and corporate executives, counsel may be forced to choose between her obligations to the corporate client and conflicting orders given by a superior; in other words, counsel may be faced with following an

**10.** *See* Model Code of Prof. Resp. EC 5-18.

**11.** *See* Model Rules of Prof. Conduct, Rule 1.13(a).

**12.** *See Restatement of the Law Governing Lawyers* § 96(1)(a).

**13.** *See* Olson, *The Potential Liabilities Faced by In-House Counsel*, 7 U. Miami Bus. L. Rev. 1, 5 (1998).

executive officer's directions or being fired from her only client.[14] To alleviate this dilemma, the general perception is that, so long as the board of directors and senior management are acting in a lawful manner, inside counsel may look to these constituents as the "spokespersons" for the corporate entity.[15]

In certain situations, however, this reliance is misplaced.[16] For instance, the Fifth Circuit in *Garner v. Wolfinbarger*,[17] in determining whether a corporation could invoke the attorney-client privilege to preclude shareholders in a derivative suit from obtaining requested documents, stated:

> "[I]t must be borne in mind that management does not manage for itself and that the beneficiaries of its action are the stockholders. Conceptualistic phrases describing the corporation as an entity separate from its stockholders are not useful tools of analysis. They serve only to obscure the fact that management has duties which run to the benefit ultimately of the stockholders.... There may be situations in which the corporate entity or its management, or both, have interests adverse to those of some or all stockholders. But when all is said and done management is not managing for itself."[18]

Additional concerns may arise from counsel's duty to inquire when offering advice. Generally, inside counsel regularly provides advice to employees and management concerning law compliance and consults with

**14.** *Id. See* Steinberg, *The Role of Inside Counsel in the 1990s: A View From Outside,* 49 SMU L. Rev. 483 (1996).

**15.** *See* Taylor, *The Role of Corporate Counsel,* 32 Rutgers L. Rev. 237, 241–246 (1979).

**16.** *See id.* at 246.

**17.** 430 F.2d 1093 (5th Cir. 1970).

**18.** *Id.* at 1101. Another issue related to client identification is whether in-house counsel may represent corporate constituents in addition to the corporate entity. Although the organization is technically the counsel's client, dual representation is generally allowed pursuant to Model Rule 1.7. *See also, infra* notes 27–30 and accompanying text. This issue is also addressed in Scenarios IV, VI herein.

management as to what steps to take when possible violations are uncovered. In this context, the question arises as to whether counsel should accept the facts as they are presented or, alternatively, whether she has a duty to inquire. Not surprisingly, the facts and circumstances of a particular situation will determine the proper course of action.[19]

Particularly when "red flags" are raised, inside counsel cannot advise on the basis of facts furnished by a corporate manager with whom he deals. In other words, certain circumstances call for a duty to inquire. If in-house counsel conducts the necessary inquiry and renders advice accordingly, it normally is implemented. However, in instances where such advice is disregarded and the situation at hand involves a crime or fraud likely to result in substantial harm to the business enterprise, counsel must take affirmative action. For example, Model Rule 1.13 provides that in-house counsel may take measures such as:

> "(1) asking for reconsideration of the matter; (2) advising that a separate legal opinion on the matter be sought for presentation to appropriate authority in the organization; and (3) referring the matter to a higher authority in the corporation, including, if warranted by the seriousness of the matter, referral to the [corporation's board of directors]."[20]

**19.** *See* Ferrara & Steinberg, *The Role of Inside Counsel in the Corporate Accountability Process,* 4 Corp. L. Rev. 3, 12 (1981); Williams, note 4 *supra.*

**20.** Model Rules of Prof. Conduct, Rule 1.13(b). Pursuant to the recently enacted Sarbanes–Oxley Act of 2002, the SEC by rule must:

> "(1) requir[e] [a subject] attorney to report evidence of a material violation of securities law or breach of fiduciary duty or similar violation by the company or any agent thereof, to the chief legal counsel or the chief executive officer of the company (or the equivalent thereof); and
>
> (2) if the counsel or officer does not appropriately respond to the evidence (adopting, as necessary, appropriate remedial measures or sanctions with respect to the violation), requir[e] [such] attorney to report the evidence to the audit committee of the board of directors of the issuer or to another committee

If the board of directors insists upon action that "is clearly a violation of law and is likely to result in substantial injury to the [corporation], the lawyer may resign. . . ."[21] Additionally, many state ethical rules permit counsel to disclose the corporate client's illegality to a shareholder or to a third party, such as a government regulatory authority (e.g., the SEC, EPA, FTC) under certain circumstances.[22]

It should be noted that resignation in such circumstances certainly is a drastic step, resulting in loss of employment, but nonetheless may be required under the ethical standards discussed above. Proceedings against attorneys brought by the Securities and Exchange Commission (SEC) illustrate this dilemma. As the SEC has pointed out, inside counsel may be charged with both ethical and supervisory responsibilities under the federal securities laws. In such circumstances, in-house counsel cannot simply advise senior management and then decline to ascertain whether such advice is being implemented. Rather, counsel must remain alert to developments and, if corrective measures are not taken, must climb the corporate ladder. If the ultimate decision-maker embodying the corporate client—the board of directors—fails to take appropriate action, counsel's practical recourse is resignation.[23]

In sum, inside counsel must be careful not to become a participant in the client's illegality.[24] Generally, provided that the client listens in good faith to the advice given, counsel should not be obligated to resign when a legitimate question exists regarding the legality

of the board of directors comprised solely of directors not employed directly or indirectly by the issuer, or to the board of directors."

**21.** *Id.* Model Rules of Prof. Conduct, Rule 1.13(c).

**22.** *See* Scenario II herein.

**23.** *See In re Gutfreund*, [1992 Transfer Binder] CCH Fed. Sec. L. Rep. ¶ 85,067 (SEC 1992); *In re Carter*, [1981 Transfer Binder] CCH Fed. Sec. L. Rep. ¶ 82,847 (SEC 1981).

**24.** *See, e.g., SEC v. National Student Mktg. Corp.*, 457 F.Supp. 682 (D.D.C.1978); Lorne & Callcott, *Administrative Actions Against Lawyers Before the SEC*, 50 Bus. Law. 1293 (1995).

of corporate conduct. In such circumstances, inside counsel's "energies should be channeled into advising and prompting corporate management and the board of directors to engage in conduct that is both legal and ethical."[25]

Another troubling issue arises when inside counsel learns that a corporate employee has allegedly violated the law. In this context, counsel may give the employee "quasi-Miranda" warnings to the effect that:

> "(a) [counsel's] role is to represent the organization; (b) an actual or potential conflict of interest may exist between the organization and the individual; (c) [counsel] cannot represent the individual; (d) their conversation may not be confidential and any information the individual provides may be used against [such individual]; and (e) he [or she] may wish to retain independent counsel."[26]

A number of inside counsel, however, argue against conveying these warnings to a suspected erring employee, reasoning that so doing is not in the corporation's interest.[27] On the other hand, failure to provide these warnings may subject counsel to increased liability exposure, particularly where the employee has a reasonable belief that counsel is personally representing the employee. For example, according to Model Rule 1.13(d), counsel has the responsibility of explaining to a non-client constituent the identity of her client (namely, that she represents the corporation) when such counsel knows or reasonably should know that the corporation's

**25.** Ferrara & Steinberg, *supra* note 19, 4 Corp. L. Rev. at 22. *See* M. Steinberg & R. Ferrara, *Securities Practice: Federal and State Enforcement* §§ 4:27–4:28 (2d ed. 2001); Millstein, *The Professional Board*, 50 Bus. Law. 1427, 1431 (1995) ("Lawyers ... understand that in most circumstances they render advice, and that taking or leaving that advice is the client's role. The limit is when the lawyer's professional responsibilities require him or her to act when the advice is ignored.").

**26.** Martin, *When Corporate Counsel Get Caught in the Middle*, Cal. Law., Dec. 1989, at 75. See Scenario IV herein.

**27.** *See, e.g.*, Aibel, *Corporate Counsel and Business Ethics: A Personal Review*, 59 Mo. L. Rev. 427, 438–439 (1994).

interests are adverse to those of such non-client constituent. Counsel also may be obligated to expressly communicate to the non-client that she does not represent such individual.[28] Failure to provide such disclosure may subject the attorney to liability for failure to warn.[29] Moreover, if the employee reasonably believes that the corporation's lawyer represents the employee personally, an attorney-client relationship may be implicated, thereby signifying that such communications between counsel and the employee may be deemed confidential.[30]

In addition to the issues arising from in-house counsel's unique employment relationship, counsel also should be aware of potential liability concerns under common and statutory (e.g., securities) law. Indeed, securities laws claims, as well as malpractice, negligent misrepresentation, aiding and abetting, and breach of fiduciary duty allegations may be of significant concern, due to in-house counsel's principal involvement in drafting key corporate documents (such as transactional documents, corporate filings, lending agreements, and legal opinions).[31] Obviously, counsel should seek to ensure that the information which she uses to draft the documents is correct. In certain situations, this objective may signify that counsel has an affirmative duty of inquiry.[32] For example, in *FDIC v. O'Melveny & Myers*,[33]

**28.** *See* Model Rules of Prof. Conduct, Rule 1.13(d).

**29.** *See Parker v. Carnahan*, 772 S.W.2d 151, 157 (Tex.App. 1989) (stating that "an attorney can be held negligent where he fails to advise a party that he is not representing him ... where the circumstances lead the party to believe that the attorney is representing him"); Scenario IV herein.

**30.** *See Westinghouse Elec. Corp. v. Kerr–McGee Corp.*, 580 F.2d 1311 (7th Cir.1978).

**31.** *See generally* Webb et al., *Understanding and Avoiding Corporate and Executive Criminal Liability*, 49 Bus. Law. 617 (1994).

**32.** Olson, *supra* note 13, 7 U. Miami Bus. L. Rev. at 32. In-house counsel may have a greater duty to inquire than outside counsel because in-house counsel have greater access to corporate information. *Id.*

**33.** 969 F.2d 744 (9th Cir. 1992), *rev'd on other grounds*, 512 U.S. 79 (1994).

a case involving counsel who had prepared securities offering documents and who had relied solely on information provided by the client company's internal participants, the Ninth Circuit held that counsel should have conducted an independent inquiry to detect and correct materially inaccurate statements.[34]

It is also important to consider in-house counsel's role within the boardroom. Generally, it is essential for counsel to comprehend the business dynamics of the enterprise and possess the acumen to understand the economics of the transaction or other matter being considered.[35] Counsel's role also encompasses the implementation of internal governance procedures to reduce the threat of subsequent litigation. In this regard, the business judgment rule serves as an impressive shield to deflect otherwise successful challenges to board action.[36]

**34.** 969 F.2d at 748–749. *See* Olson, *supra* note 13, 7 U. Miami Bus. L. Rev. at 32.

**35.** *See* Creedon, *Lawyer and Executive—The Role of the General Counsel*, 39 Bus. Law. 25 (1983); *How Agile is Your Legal Department?*, 5 Corp. Legal Times, No. 45, Aug. 1995, at 40. *See generally Symposium, Business Lawyering and Value Creation for Clients*, 74 Or. L. Rev. No. 1 (1995).

**36.** Stated succinctly, the business judgment rule has four components. First, the board of directors must focus on the issue and make a deliberative decision. Second, the board's decision must be reasonably informed. In this regard, the board should be provided with adequate information, including pertinent reports, appraisals, and other material documents central to the transaction or other matter at issue. Once having such information before it, the board should take the time necessary to reach an informed decision. Third, directors making the board's determination must be disinterested, signifying that they are not engaged in self-dealing, do not have a disproportionate financial stake in the transaction, and are not under the control or domination of a director who has such a disabling conflict of interest. Last, the decision must have a rational basis or, stated differently, must be made without gross negligence. *See, e.g., Aronson v. Lewis*, 473 A.2d 805, 812 (Del.1984); American Law Institute, *Principles of Corporate Governance: Analysis and Recommendations* § 4.01 (1994); D. Block et al., *The Business Judgment Rule: Fiduciary Duties of Corporate Directors* (4th ed. 1993 & 2001 Supp.).

In this context, process is key. If the board abides by an acceptable procedural framework, courts will be reluctant to second-guess a deliberative decision reached in good faith by a reasonably informed board.[37] Hence, inside counsel's role here is to guide the board through this process, building a fortress that will protect the decision from successful attack.

In conflict of interest transactions,[38] such as interested director transactions with a controlling shareholder, parent-subsidiary mergers, and leveraged buy-outs engineered by incumbent management, even more attention to process frequently will be necessitated. In such situations, establishment of a committee comprised of disinterested directors may be called for, as well as appointment of special counsel for the committee.[39] As decisions such as *Weinberger v. UOP, Inc.*[40] demonstrate, deficiency in process accompanied by the specter of overreaching by the control group heightens the risk that the transaction (or its terms) will be successfully challenged. To allay this prospect, participation by reasonably informed outside directors who have sufficient leverage to negotiate with the control group in an effective manner will dissuade a court from upsetting the subject transaction.[41] Playing a key role in this setting, inside counsel orchestrates the process in such a manner as to hopefully further the best interests of the corporation, shareholders, and other affected constituencies.[42]

**37.** *See ALI Principles of Corporate Governance, supra* note 36, § 4.01 & cmts.

**38.** In conflict of interest transactions, the intrinsic fairness test generally is the applicable standard. *See, e.g., Shlensky v. South Parkway Building Corp.*, 166 N.E.2d 793 (Ill.1960).

**39.** *See, e.g., Rosenblatt v. Getty Oil Co.*, 493 A.2d 929 (Del. 1985); *Weinberger v. UOP, Inc.*, 457 A.2d 701, 709 n. 7 (Del. 1983).

**40.** 457 A.2d 701 (Del.1983).

**41.** *See* M. Steinberg, *Securities Regulation: Liabilities and Remedies* § 15.04 (2002).

**42.** With respect to the interests of other constituencies, *see, e.g., Symposium, Corporate Malaise—Stakeholder Statutes: Cause or Cure?*, 21 Stetson L. Rev. No. 1 (1991). *See also*, Scenario V herein.

Inside counsel also plays a pivotal role in the practice of preventive law by establishing an effective and operational law compliance program for the subject corporation. In corporations with multifaceted operations, law compliance programs may cover such diverse areas as antitrust, environmental policies, employment and hiring practices, and securities.[43] When rendering advice with respect to law compliance, counsel may consider the following:

1. Although no system is "bullet-proof," the corporation should keep in mind that, if a violation were to occur, it would have the burden of showing that its law compliance program (Program) is reasonably effective.

2. The subject corporation's board of directors should adopt the Program, and the Program should be administered under the board's supervision as an integral part of its monitoring function. On a periodic basis, the board should review the Program for possible revision.

3. The Program's scope should reflect the nature of the enterprise's business and the legal issues such enterprise realistically may face. Given the economic practicalities involved and with the proviso that the law must be obeyed, an objective cost/benefit analysis normally is appropriate. Certainly, an enterprise engaged in several different businesses with operations abroad should be expected to develop a more extensive program than one with purely local operations specializing in a particular product market.

4. The Program (such as a Code of Conduct) should be disseminated to and understood by all affected company personnel.

**43.** American Bar Association, *Corporate Director's Guidebook* 31 (2d ed. 1994). *See* Gruner, *General Counsel in an Era of Compliance Programs and Self–Policing*, 46 Emory L.J. 1113 (1997); Reynolds, *International Antitrust Compliance for a Company with Multinational Operations,* 8 Int'l Q. 76 (1996); Steinberg & Fletcher, *Compliance Programs for Insider Trading*, 47 SMU L. Rev. 1783 (1994).

5. To integrate the Program into the corporation's culture and to help ensure continued personnel compliance, educational seminars should be conducted on a periodic basis. Moreover, consideration should be given to whether affected personnel should be required to certify annually that they have complied with the applicable Code(s) of Conduct.

6. The Program should be effectively administered. In this regard, the enterprise should not adopt any non-essential aspect of a prospective Program that it cannot feasibly implement. For example, a corporation's failure to obtain annual compliance certificates from a significant number of affected personnel may prove more harmful when such a component is contained in the corporation's Program.

7. The Program should be subject to adequate enforcement, such as spot checks, board of director (or delegated committee) review, "whistle blower" protection, and the taking of meaningful disciplinary action against those who fail to comply.[44]

In sum, inside counsel's role in helping to administer and oversee an enterprise's law compliance program is critical and may help reduce the risk of significant liability exposure. Moreover, by ensuring that the program is sufficiently comprehensive and effectively implemented, inside counsel may help ensure that the program will be deemed a mitigating factor if a violation were to occur.[45]

**44.** Steinberg, 19 Sec. Reg. L. J. 323 (1992); Aibel, *supra* note 3, 59 Mo. L. Rev. at 435–439; Pitt & Groskaufmanis, *Minimizing Corporate Civil and Criminal Liability: A Second Look at Corporate Codes of Conduct*, 78 Geo. L.J. 1559 (1990).

**45.** *Sentencing Guidelines for United States Courts*, 55 Fed. Reg. 46,600, 46,604 (1990). The federal criminal sentencing guidelines recognize that the subject corporation's establishment of an effective and operational law compliance program constitutes a mitigating factor in determining the appropriate sentence. The guidelines set forth "seven general types of steps" for such a compliance program, including effective training, monitoring, and enforcement, as well as the designation of high-level personnel with overall responsibility for

The following Scenario highlights the difficult challenges that inside counsel may have to confront.

## SCENARIO

Sylvia Gladstone, who recently left her job at a mid-size law firm in Baltimore, Maryland, is offered a position as the sole in-house attorney for Nuval Atlantic Resources, Inc. (Nuval), an Alexandria, Virginia-based company traded on the NASDAQ National Market System (NMS) with $33 million in net assets and 735 shareholders. Leaving her previous job because she was tired of the unduly long hours, counseling difficult clients, and maintaining an adequate book of business, Gladstone accepted the Nuval offer of a $185,000 salary with stock options and other key benefits. As a single mother, Gladstone is delighted with the new position and the opportunity to spend more time with her children.

Six months after being hired, Gladstone arrives at her office and finds a memo on her desk from the Chief Executive Officer (CEO) and majority shareholder of the company (52% stake), Patrick A. Whitney. The memo discusses a parcel of land located in Annandale, Virginia that Nuval purchased 12 years earlier for $565,000, and which the Company still uses as its principal warehouse. The warehouse is well situated for Nuval and aptly serves the Company's needs. Moreover, the price of the land has significantly appreciated (to around $1.8 million). In the memo, Whitney expresses his desire that Nuval sell the land (and the warehouse), realize the profit, and move the warehouse to a less expensive location. Coincidentally, Whitney personally owns a parcel of land near Wilmington, Delaware, which he purchased five years earlier for a previous (and now terminated) business venture, and which he believes would be the perfect location for Nuval's warehouse. Without

compliance. *Id.* at 46,605. *See generally* Webb & Molo, *Some Practical Considerations in Developing Effective Compliance Programs: A Framework for Meeting the Requirements of the Sentencing Guidelines*, 71 Wash. U. L.Q. 375 (1993).

disclosing the amount for which he purchased that property ($275,000), he proposes selling the property to Nuval.

While Gladstone is reading the memo, Whitney stops by her office to discuss the proposed sale. After discussing the memo's contents, Whitney adds, "I want to remind you how important this transaction is to me. I, of course, am going to recuse myself. However, I would like you to take charge of the board meeting and see this deal through. I will be upset, to use a polite word, if I don't get at least $1 million for the property."

The Board of Directors for Nuval is composed of five persons: Whitney; Whitney's daughter Lauren, who is also Treasurer and Executive Vice President; Collin Wilhelm, a friend of Whitney's and fellow member of the Crooked Tree Country Club; Roberta Razzano, a well-respected business professor at a nearby college, and Luis Rodriguez, who is a successful local entrepreneur. Neither Razzano nor Rodriguez has a business or friendship relationship with Whitney.

Gladstone is concerned about the conflicts of interest dilemmas posed by the proposed sale. Moreover, she is worried about applicable disclosure requirements, such as those set forth in Item 404 of SEC Regulation S–K.[46] Considering the circumstances, how should Gladstone present the proposed transaction to the Board of Directors? What potential problems does the situation raise? Are there any alternative solutions?

**46.** Item 404 of SEC Regulation S–K requires disclosure of transactions with the corporation by: (1) directors; (2) director-nominees; (3) executive officers; (4) five percent shareholders; and (5) members of the immediate family of the primary reporting persons involving more than $60,000 made within the past year in which such persons have a direct or indirect material interest. *See* Item 404, Regulation S–K, *as adopted*, SEC Securities Exchange Act Release No. 19290 (1982). This proposed transaction, if consummated, would be required to be disclosed under Item 404.

*

# Scenario X

# COUNSEL AS DIRECTOR?

The practice of the general counsel serving as a corporate director to a business enterprise, whether that person is an in-house lawyer or a partner in a law firm, has been widespread for decades. From the client's perspective, the specialized training, unique experience, and analytical skills of its corporate counsel are a valued resource to a board of directors when making business decisions.[1] Additionally, attorneys see this dual role as a means of strengthening the relationship with their clients as well as a way to help ensure continued legal business and financial stability for their law firms. Indeed, with the weakening of long-term relationships and the intense competition for retaining corporate representation in recent years, the solidification of this relationship is paramount.[2]

Although the practice of corporate counsel serving as director remains relatively common, the propriety of attorneys acting in this dual capacity has long been criticized. Because an attorney/director must play dual

**1.** *See* Carrey, *Corporate Lawyer/Corporate Director: A Compromise of Professional Independence,* 67 N.Y. St. B.J. at 6 (Nov. 1995); Kim, *Dual Identities and Dueling Obligations: Preserving Independence in Corporate Representations*, 68 Tenn. L. Rev. 179 (2001).

**2.** *See* Cheek & Lamar, *Lawyers as Directors of Clients: Conflicts of Interest, Potential Liability and Other Pitfalls*, PLI No. B4–6940, 712 PLI/Corp. 461, 463–464 (1990).

roles as counsel and director, this arrangement raises a variety of issues pertaining to professional responsibility, potential conflicts of interest, and enhanced liability exposure.

For example, the application of the attorney-client privilege will be assessed on an ad-hoc basis depending upon whether the attorney/director was acting as legal counsel or as a director. By assuming this dual function, therefore, the corporation's assertion of the attorney-client privilege may be subject to siege.[3] Also, by serving as director, counsel incurs the risk of having diminished ability to exercise independent judgment in general.

In these dual roles, counsel has a conflict between being a "team player" while at the same time rendering dispassionate legal advice that will be received with respect and without hostility by the inside directors.[4] Moreover, the attorney/director may be denied legal malpractice insurance coverage by the carrier on the basis that the alleged impropriety did not involve the practice of law. Further, when counsel steps out of his or her attorney's shoes and acts as director, counsel's personal liability exposure is magnified. In such circumstances, courts frequently apply enhanced standards to analyze the propriety of the alleged wrongdoing.[5] In-

**3.** *Grimes v. LCC International, Inc.*, 1999 WL 252381 (Del.Ch.1999). *See* M. Steinberg, *Corporate and Securities Malpractice* 251 (1992); Finklestein et al., *Attorney–Client Privilege: Potential Dangers of Having Corporate General Counsel Perform Multiple Roles*, 33 Rev. Sec. & Comm. Reg. 49 (2000).

**4.** *See* Model Rules of Prof. Conduct, Rule 1.7 cmt. 35; Hershman, *Special Problems of Inside Counsel for Financial Institutions*, 33 Bus. Law. 1435, 1439–1440 (1978); Lorne, *The Corporate and Securities Adviser, the Public Interest, and Professional Ethics*, 76 Mich. L. Rev. 425, 490–495 (1978); Riger, *The Lawyer–Director—A Vexing Problem*, 33 Bus. Law. 2381 (1978).

An inside director generally is one who has a significant employment relationship, such as being an executive officer of the corporation.

**5.** *See, e.g., Escott v. BarChris Constr. Corp.*, 283 F.Supp. 643 (S.D.N.Y.1968); Hershman, *supra* note 4, 33 Bus. Law. at 1440 (asserting that "as a director, the General Counsel is likely to be held to a higher standard of care than other di-

deed, it has been asserted that lawyers who agree to sit as directors "have to be 'certifiably nuts' because of the likelihood of being sued."[6]

Despite the potential risks, however, many corporations exhort corporate counsel to serve as a director, due to perceived advantages that accrue to the client corporation. A primary benefit is the opportunity for the lawyer to be well informed concerning the corporation's affairs and to be in a position to provide legal advice when contemplated actions are first presented or when problematic situations initially arise.[7] This enables counsel to be more effective in rendering advice to the board of directors, thereby preventing problems which could arise "due to the failure of the company to consult the attorney before taking an action or due to the . . . failure of management or the board of directors to recognize developing legal problems in their early stages."[8]

Because the attorney/director understands the legal implications of a potential decision, she can also act as a sounding board for corporate management.[9] This facilitates the flow of information between the board of directors and counsel because the attorney is more closely involved in the affairs of the client and is aware of the critical issues facing management.[10] Additionally,

rectors because of his [or her] unique access to information and expertise").

**6.** *Lawyer–Directors Are Key Targets for Plaintiffs' Lawyers, ABA Group Told*, 21 Sec. Reg. & L. Rep. (BNA) 1272 (1989) (hereinafter "*Lawyer–Directors*").

**7.** *See* Thurston, *Corporate Counsel on the Board of Directors: An Overview*, 10 Cumb. L. Rev. 791, 792 (1980) (citing Forrow, *Special Problems of Inside Counsel for Industrial Companies*, 33 Bus. Law. 1453, 1461 (1978); Hawes, *Should Counsel to a Corporation be Barred From Serving as a Director?—A Personal View*, 1 Corp. L. Rev. 14, 17 (1978)).

**8.** Thurston, *supra* note 7, 10 Cumb. L. Rev. at 792.

**9.** *Id.* at 793. *See also, The Corporate Director's Guidebook*, 33 Bus. Law. 1591, 1607 (1978).

**10.** Thurston, *supra* note 7, 10 Cumb. L. Rev. at 793. *See* Cheek & Lamar, *supra* note 2, at 464; Zaffirini, *The Challenges of Serving as an Attorney/Director*, 33 Tex. J. Bus. Law No. 3, at 43, 44–45 (Fall 1996).

because the attorney/director, like the other board members, is subject to the same potential for liability as a director, the other directors may have greater comfort in the legal advice rendered by the attorney.[11]

From the law firm's perspective, economic necessities may dictate counsel serving as a director. An attorney's dual role enhances the relationship with clients and promotes continued legal business for the firm. Indeed, in some situations, senior executive officers may feel strongly that general counsel should be an integral member of the "team," thereby insisting that such counsel serve on the board. To maintain the corporation as a client generating substantial legal fees, outside counsel may acquiesce in this arrangement.[12]

In general, applicable ethical rules contain no specific prohibition against an attorney serving as a corporate director. In fact, the only guidance offered by the ABA Model Rules is included in the commentary to Model Rule 1.7, which touches upon the potential conflicts of interest that may exist when counsel serves as a director of the corporate client. Specifically, the Comment states:

> "A lawyer for a corporation or other organization who is also a member of its board of directors should determine whether the responsibilities of the two roles may conflict.... If there is material risk that the dual role will compromise the lawyer's independence of professional judgment, the lawyer should not serve as a director or should cease to act as the corporation's lawyer when conflicts of interest arise...."[13]

**11.** Thurston, *supra* note 7, 10 Cumb. L. Rev. at 793; Zaffirini, *supra* note 10, 33 Tex. J. Bus. Law No. 3, at 45.

**12.** *See* Lorne, *supra* note 4, 76 Mich. L. Rev. at 490–495.

**13.** Model Rules of Prof. Conduct, Rule 1.7 cmt 35. *See* Committee Report, *The Lawyer as Director of a Client*, 57 Bus. Law. 387 (2001) (stating that "[t]here is no ethical prohibition against a lawyer serving as a director of a client").

Likewise, the American Law Institute's Restatement of the Law Governing Lawyers generally acquiesces in the counsel-director arrangement:

> "A lawyer's duties as counsel can conflict with the lawyer's duties arising from the lawyer's service as a director or officer of a corporate client. Simultaneous service as corporate lawyer and corporate director or officer is not forbidden by this Section.... However, when the obligations or personal interests as director are materially adverse to those of the lawyer as corporate counsel, the lawyer may not continue to serve as corporate counsel without the informed consent of the corporate client."[14]

A 1998 formal ethics opinion issued by the American Bar Association[15] provides additional suggestions to help an attorney/director avoid ethical violations and other problems. For example, the ABA opinion states that an attorney/director should:

> "Reasonably assure that management and the board of directors understand: (i) the different responsibilities of legal counsel and director; (ii) that when acting as legal counsel, the lawyer represents only the corporate entity and not its individual officers and directors; and (iii) that at times conflicts of interest may arise under the rules governing lawyers' conduct that may cause the lawyer to recuse herself as a director or to recommend engaging other independent counsel to represent the corporation in the matter, or to serve as co-counsel with the lawyer or her firm."[16]

**14.** *Restatement of the Law Governing Lawyers* § 135 cmt. d.

**15.** *Lawyer Serving as Director of Client Corporation*, ABA Comm. on Ethics and Professional Responsibility, Formal Op. 98–410 (1998).

**16.** *Id. See* Task Force on the Independent Lawyer, ABA Section of Litigation, *The Lawyer–Director: Implications for Independence* (1998); Committee Report, *supra* note 13, 57 Bus. Law. at 387–395; Kim, *supra* note 1, 68 Tenn. L. Rev. at 219–246.

Nevertheless, as the following discussion illustrates, serving as an attorney/director remains fraught with risk, including (1) the potential loss of the attorney-client privilege; (2) potential conflict of interest challenges and the perceived loss of independence; (3) a heightened duty of care; (4) increased liability risk under the securities laws;[17] (5) possible disqualification of the attorney's law firm; (6) vicarious liability for the attorney's law firm; (7) and possible loss of liability insurance coverage.

The first principal area of risk is the potential loss of the attorney-client privilege.[18] In general, the purpose of the attorney-client privilege is to encourage full and frank communication between attorneys and their clients and thereby promote broader public interests in the observance of law.[19] In order to invoke the privilege while acting as both attorney and director, an attorney must render the advice in her role as a lawyer, rather than in her role as a director. If the information in question was communicated in the role as director, the privilege may be lost. However, although most attorney/directors regularly render business advice as well as

**17.** An attorney/director faces increased liability risk under both federal and state securities laws. For purposes of this illustration, this Scenario focuses on federal securities laws.

**18.** The attorney-client privilege is discussed in Scenario IV herein. In *United States v. United Shoe Machinery Co.*, 89 F.Supp. 357, 358–359 (D.Mass. 1950), the court set forth the following definition of the attorney-client privilege:

> "The privilege applies only if (1) the asserted holder of the privilege is or sought to become a client; (2) the person to whom the communication was made (a) is a member of the bar of a court, or his subordinate and (b) in connection with this communication is acting as a lawyer; (3) the communication relates to a fact of which the attorney was informed (a) by his client (b) without the presence of strangers (c) for the purpose of securing primarily either (i) an opinion on law or (ii) legal services or (iii) assistance in some legal proceeding, and not (d) for the purpose of committing a crime or tort; and (4) the privilege has been (a) claimed and (b) not waived by the client."

**19.** *Upjohn Co. v. United States*, 449 U.S. 383, 389 (1981). *See* Scenario IV *supra*.

legal advice, no clear test has been articulated to determine the issue of whether an attorney is acting as a director or as an attorney. Instead, courts traditionally have used a factual analysis.[20] For example, in *United States v. Vehicular Parking, Ltd.*,[21] the defendant in an antitrust case attempted to invoke the attorney-client privilege with respect to certain communications involving an attorney/director. The court, however, concluded that as a director, the attorney was involved in the promotion and management of the company so that "his communications involving business, rather than legal, advice [were], therefore, not privileged."[22]

When an attorney/director performs dual roles, instances also may arise where an attorney's interests as counsel conflict with her duties as director. For example, one potential conflict of interest involves fee considerations—the attorney's self-interest in the corporation's continued retention of her law firm may conflict with her fiduciary duties as director.[23] Law firm revenues generated from these fees may place pressure on the firm and the attorney/director to maintain the relationship, and may make counsel reluctant to voice disapproval of certain actions.[24]

Related to these concerns is the issue of whether an attorney, who serves on the board of directors of a corporation which has a significant relationship with the attorney's firm, is considered "independent" for certain analyses involving the business judgment rule.[25] Gener-

**20.** Thurston, *supra* note 7, 10 Cumb. L. Rev. at 811.

**21.** 52 F.Supp. 751 (D.Del. 1943).

**22.** *Id.* at 753–754. *See SEC v. Gulf & Western Ind., Inc.*, 518 F.Supp. 675 (D.D.C.1981); *Federal Savings & Loan Ins. Corp. v. Fielding*, 343 F.Supp. 537 (D.Nev.1972); Thurston, *supra* note 7, Cumb. L. Rev. at 811.

**23.** Gould, *Should Lawyers Serve as Directors of Corporations For Which They Act as Counsel?*, 1978 Utah L. Rev. 711, 714 (1978).

**24.** *See* Cheek & Lamar, *supra* note 2, at 470.

**25.** *See* Harris & Valihura, *Outside Counsel as Director: The Pros and Potential Pitfalls of Dual Service*, 53 Bus. Law. 479, 489 (1998). The business judgment rule provides an impressive shield from liability for directors, so long as they are

ally, one of the rule's requirements is that subject directors making a board's determination must be disinterested, signifying that they are not engaged in self-dealing, do not have a disproportionate financial stake in the transaction, and are not under the control or domination of a director who has such a disabling conflict of interest.[26] An attorney/director, however, may promote the appearance of self-interest when voting on corporate action that would likely involve significant legal work for his law firm, or taking part in board discussions focusing on whether to reject the prospective sale of a particular corporate division which has generated substantial legal fees for his firm in the past. This appearance of impropriety is illustrated in *Steiner v. Meyerson.*[27] There, a director's law firm earned close to $1 million in revenues in representing the corporation. The court found that "[r]ealism .... requires one to acknowledge the possibility that a [law firm] partner bringing in close to $1 million in revenues from a single client in one year may be sufficiently beholden to, or at least significantly influenced by, that client as to affect the independence of his judgment."[28]

Due to an attorney/director's direct involvement in the activities of the corporation, there is also a greater risk for disqualification of the attorney and the attorney's firm in certain instances. Disqualification, for example, may occur if a plaintiff brings a lawsuit naming as defendants all of the directors, including the attorney/director. In this situation, the individual directors

disinterested, reasonably informed, have no disabling conflict of interest, and the decision made is rational. Gross negligence is the applicable standard for a plaintiff to hurdle in order to rebut the presumption of the business judgment rule. *See Aronson v. Lewis*, 473 A.2d 805 (Del.1984).

**26.** *See Aronson v. Lewis*, 473 A.2d 805 (Del.1984); *Sinclair Oil Corp. v. Levien,* 280 A.2d 717 (Del.1971); *Shlensky v. South Parkway Bldg. Corp.*, 166 N.E.2d 793 (Ill.1960).

**27.** [1995 Transfer Binder] CCH Fed. Sec. L. Rep. ¶ 98,857 (Del.Ch.1995).

**28.** *Id.* at 93,152. *See* Harris & Valihura, *supra* note 25, 53 Bus. Law. at 489.

may utilize a "reliance on counsel" defense, which would conflict with the attorney/director's position that she relied on information provided to her by the other board members.[29] Similarly, a court may disqualify an attorney/director from representing the client corporation when the attorney/director is called as a witness. The court in *Cottonwood Estates v. Paradise Builders*,[30] for instance, disqualified an attorney/director, stating:

> "This case demonstrates that [serving in a dual role as officer and attorney for a corporation] is fraught with danger. A lawyer owes his client a duty of loyalty and duty to exercise independent professional judgment. A lawyer representing a corporation has a duty to the corporate entity which may or may not be coexistent with any duty owed the board of directors or officers. Here, the lawyer is being called into court to answer for his acts as an officer where his corporate ministerial duties conflicted with his professional duty to exercise independent judgment on behalf of his client."[31]

Additionally, Rule 3.7 of the ABA Model Rules of Professional Conduct, with certain exceptions, provides that a "lawyer shall not act as advocate at a trial in which the lawyer is likely to be a necessary witness."[32] Moreover, an attorney/director's law firm may be disqualified from representing the client corporation if it files for bankruptcy. Section 327(a) of the Bankruptcy Code "requires that an attorney retained by a corporation filing for protection under the Code be a 'disinterested person,'[33] which is defined to exclude anyone who

**29.** Thurston, *supra* note 7, 10 Cumb. L. Rev. at 808.

**30.** 624 P.2d 296 (Ariz. 1981).

**31.** *Id.* at 303. *See* Model Rules of Prof. Conduct, Rule 3.7; Cheek & Lamar, *supra* note 2, at 488–489.

**32.** Model Rules of Professional Conduct, Rule 3.7. *See* Block, Meierholfer, & Wallach, *Lawyers Serving on the Boards of Directors of Clients: A Survey of the Problems*, 7 Insights No. 4, at 3, 4–5 (April 1993).

**33.** 11 U.S.C. § 327(a).

has been a director or officer of the corporation within two years of the filing for reorganization."[34]

When an attorney serves as a director, he may be required to exercise a higher standard of care than that of certain other directors, thus resulting in greater personal liability exposure. In general, Section 8.30 of the Model Business Corporation Act requires that directors "discharg[e] their duties with the care that a person in a like position would reasonably believe appropriate under similar circumstances"[35] Developments in corporate and securities law signify, however, that attorney/directors must not only act with the due care ordinarily required of outside directors,[36] but also must adhere to higher standards premised on the attorney/director's unique skills and legal expertise—or in other words, the standard expected of an "ordinarily prudent attorney/director."[37]

A widely cited case dealing with the issue of an attorney/director's duty of care (also called "due diligence" in certain contexts) is *Escott v. BarChris Construction Corp.*[38] In *BarChris,* the plaintiffs brought an action for damages under Section 11 of the Securities Act of 1933 against the company, its officers, directors, accountants, and underwriters, alleging that the company's registration statement contained materially false and misleading statements. One defendant in the suit was the outside counsel for BarChris who was a director of the company, and whose law firm was the principal drafter of the registration statement at issue. Although

**34.** Block, Meierholfer & Wallach, *supra* note 32, 7 Insights No. 4, at 5; 11 U.S.C. § 101(13)(A), (D).

**35.** Model Bus. Corp. Act § 8.30(b).

**36.** Outside directors generally are defined as those directors who neither are employees nor have any other significant relationship with the corporation. A more lax definition would render any non-employee director to be an outside director. *See The Corporate Director's Guidebook,* 33 Bus. Law. 1595 (1978).

**37.** Cheek & Lamar, *supra* note 2, at 490–491.

**38.** 283 F.Supp. 643 (S.D.N.Y.1968).

the claims against him concerned solely his role as a director, the court held:

> "[I]n considering [the defendant's] due diligence defenses, the unique position which he occupied cannot be disregarded. As the director most directly concerned with writing the registration statement and assuring its accuracy, more was required of him in the way of reasonable investigation than could fairly be expected of a director who had no connection with this work."[39]

In *Feit v. Leasco Data Processing Equipment Corp.*,[40] another case involving the attorney/director's due diligence defense under Section 11, the court opined that an attorney/director must undertake the strict investigatory obligations of an "inside" director. The court reasoned that the attorney-director was "so intimately involved in this registration process that to treat him as anything but an insider would involve a gross distortion of the realities of [the corporation's] management."[41] Supporting *BarChris*, the court stated that what constitutes satisfaction of a director's duty will vary with "the degree of involvement of the individual, his expertise and his access to the pertinent information and data [and] [w]hat is reasonable for one director may not be reasonable for another by virtue of their differing positions."[42] Thus, under the standards outlined in the Model Business Corporation Act and as enunciated in such cases as *BarChris* and *Feit*, attorney/directors are required to both perform a higher quality investigation and to act in a more prudent manner. Consequently, the attorney/director "is measured by a higher standard

**39.** *Id.* at 690. Under Section 11, except for the issuer which is strictly liable, all defendants have a due diligence defense. *See* M. Steinberg, *Understanding Securities Law* 160–172 (3d ed. 2001).

**40.** 332 F.Supp. 544 (E.D.N.Y.1971).

**41.** *Id.* at 576. *See* Block, Meierholfer & Wallach, *supra* note 32, 7 Insights No. 4, at 6.

**42.** 332 F. Supp. at 577–578. *See* Cheek & Lamar, *supra* note 2, at 495.

that takes into account his 'superior knowledge of, and access to, the relevant information.' "[43]

Attorney/directors also may be held liable under the securities laws for "causing" a subject violation.[44] Attorney/directors should be especially wary of these provisions because their dual roles make them more vulnerable to being sued for "causing" a securities law violation.[45] For example, in an enforcement proceeding brought against George C. Kern, Jr.,[46] the SEC alleged that Kern, as a director and the outside counsel of Allied Stores Corporation, "caused" that company's violation of the tender offer disclosure requirements during a hostile takeover.[47] Another proceeding, *In the Matter of Costanza,*[48] involved an attorney who served as bond counsel for Orange County, California in eight bond offerings. In its cease-and-desist order, the SEC

**43.** Thurston, *supra* note 7, 10 Cumb. L. Rev. at 821, *quoting*, Folk, *Civil Liabilities Under the Federal Securities Acts: The BarChris Case*, 55 Va. L. Rev. 1, 34–35 (1969). For a more recent case recognizing that an attorney/director may be held to a higher standard of care *see, e.g., In re Rospatch Securities Litigation,* [1992 Transfer Binder] CCH Fed. Sec. L. Rep. ¶ 96,939 (W.D.Mich.1992) ("In these circumstances, [the attorney's] knowledge as a director cannot be separated from the knowledge of his law firm. In addition, the lawyer-director may also be held to a higher standard of care."). In addition to the risks arising under Section 11 of the Securities Act, attorney/directors also may face greater liability risks under the antifraud provisions of the federal securities laws.

**44.** *See, e.g.,* Section 15(c)(4) of the Securities Exchange Act (a person who was a "cause" of a failure to comply with the Exchange Act's reporting, proxy, or tender offer rules may be subject to an administrative enforcement action); Section 21(C)(a) of the Securities Exchange Act (cease or desist order may be imposed on a person who was a "cause" of the violation).

**45.** *See* Block, Meierholfer & Wallach, *supra* note 32, 7 Insights No. 4, at 6.

**46.** *In re Kern,* [1988–1989 Transfer Binder] CCH Fed. Sec. L. Rep. ¶ 84,342 (ALJ 1988), *aff'd on other grounds*, [1991 Transfer Binder] CCH Fed. Sec. L. Rep. ¶ 84,815 (SEC 1991).

**47.** *Id. See* Albert, *The Lawyer–Director: An Oxymoron?,* 9 Geo. J. Leg. Eth. 413, 460 (1996); Cheek & Lamar, *supra* note 2, at 500.

**48.** Securities Act Release No. 7621 (1999).

alleged that Costanza omitted material information in the official statements for the offerings, which she assisted in preparing and reviewing. The SEC charged her with violating Section 17(a)(2) and 17(a)(3) of the Securities Act and found that she "knew or should have known" that the official statements omitted material information.[49]

An attorney/director also faces problems involving insurance coverage—in the event that an attorney/director becomes involved in litigation, there exists a distinct possibility that she will be denied coverage.[50] This is a significant concern because an attorney/director is more likely to be the target of a malpractice claim. Indeed, according to one commentator, an attorney/director is "an irresistible target for plaintiffs . . . even when there is no evidence of legal malpractice in the usual sense because lawyers and law firms usually maintain large professional liability insurance policies."[51]

Generally, an attorney/director has insurance coverage under two different types of policies: (1) professional liability insurance procured by the attorney/director's law firm (which insures the law firm and its attorneys against liabilities arising from the providing of legal services); and (2) directors' and officers' (D & O) liability insurance procured by the subject corporation (which insures the director from liability resulting from such person's conduct in her directorial capacity).[52]

Because the demarcation between professional advice as counsel and business conduct as director is not clear cut, the risk arises that an attorney/director will be denied coverage under the company's D & O insurance

**49.** *See id.*

**50.** *See* Block, Meierholfer & Wallach, *supra* note 32, 7 Insights No. 4, at 8.

**51.** Albert, *supra* note 47, 9 Geo. J. Leg. Eth. at 463 (citations omitted).

**52.** Block, Meierholfer & Wallach, *supra* note 32, 7 Insights No. 4, at 8; Cheek & Lamar, *supra* note 2, at 499.

policy as well as the law firm's professional liability insurance policy.[53] Indeed, because professional liability insurance generally provides coverage for acts, errors, and omissions in the rendering of professional services while acting as legal counsel, the insurer may deny coverage by asserting that the attorney/director's conduct was outside the scope of her role as counsel. On the other hand, the D & O insurer may contend that the actions of the attorney/director were not within the purview of her obligations as a director. Therefore, it is distinctly possible that an attorney/director will not have coverage under either policy.[54]

Due to an increasing number of lawsuits against law firms of attorney/directors that relate to the conduct of one of their lawyers on a corporation's board of directors, a law firm may similarly face enhanced liability exposure. For instance, an attorney/director's law firm may be at greater risk for malpractice and negligent misrepresentation claims. Similarly, the law firm may be sued for controlling person liability under the securities laws as well as under the common law doctrine of respondeat superior.[55] Such claims are not surprising, because, as observed by one commentator, the attorney/director relationship ties the board of directors

**53.** *See* sources note 52 *supra.*

**54.** *Id.*

**55.** Section 20(a) of the Securities Exchange Act extends liability, subject to a good faith and noninducement defense, to anyone who "controls" another person that violates the Act or any rule thereunder. Although the term "control" is not defined in the Securities Acts, the SEC has defined the term to include "the possession, directly or indirectly, of the power to cause the direction of management and policies of a person." *See* Rule 405, 17 C.F.R. § 230.405. If control is established, the burden shifts to the defendant to show that it acted in good faith and did not induce the primary violation. *See In re Rospatch, Inc. Securities Litigation*, [1992 Transfer Binder] CCH Fed. Sec. L. Rep. ¶ 96,939 (W.D.Mich.1992), (upholding a control person claim against a defendant attorney and his law firm where the attorney was a director of the corporation, served on the board committees, and he and his firm were heavily involved in the corporation's affairs). *See also*, M. Steinberg, *Securities Regulation* 740–745 (3d ed. 1998).

to the law firm and to the law firm's malpractice policy—a "very attractive" prospect for a plaintiff lawyer looking at a troubled company.[56]

Because of the enhanced risk of liability exposure, law firms should carefully assess whether to adopt a policy concerning their attorneys serving as directors on client boards. When implementing such a policy, a law firm should "carefully address all pertinent considerations, including those factors discussed above, to determine whether the attorney, the law firm, and the corporate client will be best served by such representation; and if so, what safeguards should be observed."[57]

Various commentators have suggested that law firms divide responsibilities between attorney/directors and other lawyers of the firm in such a manner that potential conflicts of interest and imputed liability claims are minimized.[58] One such way would be to erect a "wall"—precluding the attorney/director from performing any legal work for the corporate client, or removing him from participating in the billing process of such client.[59] Both approaches seek to minimize the connection between the lawyer's role as counsel and his role as director, thereby helping to avert vicarious liability claims and alleged conflicts of interest.[60] The use of such "walls," however, poses problems. First, the "walls" do not entirely eliminate the risk of conflicts of interest—although the attorney/director would not know precisely the extent to which his law firm is profiting from its relationship with the corporate-client, he would certainly be aware that the firm is benefiting

**56.** *See "Lawyer–Directors," supra* note 6, at 1272.

**57.** Parker et al., *Law Firm Liability Under the Federal Securities Laws*, 6 Insights No. 3, at 19, 22 (March 1992).

**58.** *See, e.g.,* Zaffirini, *supra* note 10, 33 Tex. J. Bus. Law. at 53.

**59.** *Id.* The concept of creating a "wall" first arose in the area of attorney disqualification. See Scenario VII herein.

**60.** Zaffirini, *supra* note 10, 33 Tex. J. Bus. Law. at 53. *See* Parker, *supra* note 57, 6 Insights No. 3, at 23.

in a significant way.[61] These "walls" also may impair the attorney-client privilege, given that their implementation may evidence that the attorney/director's role principally is business-related.[62]

A better alternative may be for counsel, rather than serving as a director, to attend all board of director and key committee meetings and meaningfully participate only in an attorney role. This route enables counsel to be informed and to provide advice as appropriate, but without losing her independence and facing the burdens accompanying a directorship. Indeed, this view was espoused by former SEC Chairman Harold Williams, who stated:

> "I am not convinced that it is possible to develop a conduct rule which adequately resolves the inherent conflicts in dual service.... I would suggest, however, that there is no impediment to having general counsel attend board meetings as an active participant. I believe it should be standard practice. Such a procedure would give the company and the board the benefits of counsel, without presenting the dilemma posed by dual service."[63]

The following Scenario highlights many of the ethical issues and potential liability concerns that arise from the counsel/director dilemma.

## SCENARIO

Leon McIntyre, after traveling west to attend law school at UCLA, returned to his home town, Cleveland Ohio, to practice law. After learning the ropes in the corporate law section of a large Cleveland firm for five years, two of McIntyre's colleagues, both senior associates, and McIntyre leave the mega firm to start their own law firm called Haynes, McIntyre & Wallenstein,

**61.** *See* Zaffirini, *supra* note 10, 33 Tex. Bus. Law. at 53.

**62.** *Id.* at 54.

**63.** Williams, *The Role of Inside Counsel in Corporate Accountability*, [1979–1980 Transfer Binder] CCH Fed. Sec. L. Rep. ¶ 82,318, at 82,375 (1979).

P.C. As anticipated, after six months, billables and collectibles are weak, yet fortunately, are improving. McIntyre thereupon is approached by Sy Lucas, who he knew somewhat in high school and with whom he has become better acquainted in their church activities. Lucas is the chief executive officer of a publicly held company named Lukomas.com (the "Company"), the common stock of which is traded on the NASDAQ Small Cap Market.

Lucas informs McIntyre that the Company, which employs one in-house attorney, is looking for a law firm to be its outside general counsel and would like McIntyre's law firm to serve in that role. Lucas estimates that fees should approach $50,000 annually, if not more, and that a secondary public stock offering is tentatively planned two years from now which also should generate significant fees for McIntyre's firm (which would serve as the Company's counsel in that prospective offering). As a condition to this arrangement, Lucas explains that Lukomas.com needs a fifth director and that McIntyre must be that director. Without McIntyre's agreement to this proposition, Lucas tells McIntyre that the Company will retain another law firm to be its general counsel.

Should McIntyre and his law firm (Haynes, McIntyre & Wallenstein, P.C.) agree to represent Lukomas.com under the conditions set forth by Lucas? What, if any, diligence should be conducted by McIntyre and the law firm regarding Lukomas.com and its key executives, including Lucas? Does McIntyre's prospective dual role as counsel for the Company and as corporate director raise ethical as well as potential liability concerns?

*

# Appendix

## ENGAGEMENT LETTER

## (EXAMPLE 1)

Jagger Starr & Houston, P.C.
Seven Citrus Grove
37th Floor
Miami, Florida 33058

May 20, 2002

Mr. Leonard J. Monroe
Monroe Enterprises, L.L.C.
Three Tropicana Lane
Fort Lauderdale, Florida
33317

Dear Mr. Monroe:

We appreciate your confidence in Jagger Starr & Houston, P.C. and your decision to retain our firm to provide legal advice and representation. We believe the attorney-client relationship is best served by a clear understanding of the scope and financial terms of our engagement. The purpose of this letter is to set forth that understanding.

*Identity of Client and Scope of Engagement:*

We have been retained to provide the following legal services to Monroe Enterprises, L.L.C. ("the Company") in connection with litigation brought by Abso–Duet Corporation against the Company pending in Broward County, Florida.

If we undertake, at your request, additional legal work in the future for the Company, this letter will continue to define our relationship unless we enter into a subsequent letter agreement for that work. Once the work described herein (or any additional legal work we have undertaken at your request) has been completed, our engagement will end and, absent a specific request, we will have no further responsibility to advise you about changes in the law or later actions to be taken.

*Billing, Administration and Work Assignments:*

We try to take into account all relevant factors in setting our fees and related charges. The principal factor is the hourly rate, which is set in accordance with the seniority, expertise, and location of the lawyer or paralegal performing a given task.

Our policy with respect to our billing and fee arrangements, the assignment of additional lawyers and other pertinent matters are set forth in the attached Standard Terms of Engagement. Those provisions will apply unless this letter otherwise specifically addresses an issue.

We will bill you for expenses associated with your representation. These expenses—such as internal copying, computer research, telephone calls and air courier—will be billed on a cost basis absent a mark-up. Our internal costs for the aforementioned are reviewed periodically and adjusted to reflect changes in our cost structure.

We request advance payment for the work we anticipate performing. Our fees and charges for the work will be applied against this advance payment, and appropriate credit will be reflected on the statements you receive. Based on our analysis of the work to be performed, we believe a $25,000 advance payment is appropriate. The unearned portion of the advance, if any, will be refunded to you after this engagement has been completed. This prepayment of legal fees will be kept in an escrow account and drawn therefrom as invoices are rendered. If the need arises, we may request replenishment of this account.

We may contract with outside vendors to provide certain services associated with your representation, e.g., copying services. In such instances, we may bill you for such services prior to actually paying the vendor and/or pay the vendor upon receipt of your payment. Before proceeding, however, we would provide full disclosure as to the arrangement and obtain your consent. (See "Standard Terms of Engagement"—Disbursements and Charges)

*Litigation Support Services:*

As part of our engagement, we will provide the following litigation support services. First, we will provide optical scanning of all pleadings and correspondence at no cost to you. Second, we will provide optical scanning of all documents obtained through discovery for $0.18 per page. Third, we will provide coding for these documents which captures essential information about each document for $45.00 per hour. Fourth, we employ a litigation support technology specialist who will supervise litigation support services for this Matter, such as database development, input, retrieval and categorization of data and evidence for all legal and discovery proceedings, and preparation of electronic displays using Powerpoint or similar software for hearings and trial at an hourly rate of $95.00. We believe this represents a substantial savings for our clients since this work is frequently performed by paralegals charging considerably higher rates.

*Conflicts of Interest:*

We have procedures designed to avoid acceptance of engagements that would create a conflict of interest. Based on the information you provided, we have reviewed our records and have discovered no conflict that would preclude our representation of you in the engagement described in this letter. Please note that unless a subsidiary or other affiliate is described herein as a client, we do not consider such subsidiary or other affiliate to be our client in determining conflicts of interest or for any other purpose.

It is possible that a new or existing client might seek our advice or representation in a matter that involves you, directly or indirectly. Under the various codes of professional responsibility that govern the practice of law, a lawyer may not represent a client in a matter that is directly adverse to the interests of another existing client, absent informed consent. Competing economic interests are not, however, matters of direct adversity, and we would, therefore, be free to accept such other engagements without your consent.

We may be asked to accept an engagement that is considered to be in direct conflict with our engagement with you. If so, if we determine that (i) we would not be hindered in continuing to represent your interests in a fair and aggressive manner, (ii) our representation of you will not be adversely affected by undertaking the new engagement, *or* (iii) our independent professional judgment will not be materially limited by undertaking the new engagement, *and* (iv) the new engagement would not involve the use or disclosure of any confidential information about you, and if you concur in our judgment, after full disclosure, on those issues, we would hope that you would consent to the other engagement.

If the terms of this letter are satisfactory, please sign a copy in the space provided, and return it to me with the advance payment of $25,000. We appreciate the opportunity to be of service to you.

Very truly yours,

____________________________

Luis M. Salazar

Agreed:
Monroe Enterprises, L.L.C.

By: ______________________
Leonard J. Monroe

Enclosure

*Jagger Starr & Houston, P.C.—Standard Terms of Engagement*

*FEES.* Unless a specific alternate fee arrangement is set forth in the engagement letter, our fees are calculated based upon the fair value for the services we render after taking into consideration many factors, including but not limited to the complexity or novelty of the work performed; the seniority, experience, practice area and location of the lawyers, paralegals or law clerks performing the work; the time period within which the work is required to be completed; the likelihood that the engagement will preclude our acceptance of other employment; the number of hours required to perform the work; the nature and length of our professional relationship with the Client; the results obtained; and the fees charged for similar services. Hourly rates (determined using the forgoing factors) are established for lawyers, paralegals, law clerks, and other staff timekeepers, both for our internal cost accounting records and for matters where we have agreed to base our fees primarily or exclusively on the number of hours worked. Those base rates are adjusted periodically, in light of the factors enumerated above, as well as cost of living and market considerations.

*WORK ASSIGNMENTS.* The lawyer with whom the Client deals primarily may assign responsibility for completing some of the Client's work to other lawyers or personnel in the firm under his or her supervision, and may use other firm lawyers where specialized help is needed. The supervising lawyer will continue to be responsible for the Client's engagement, however. We assign tasks among lawyers, paralegals, and law clerks to produce the highest quality work in the most efficient and cost-effective manner. Our firm functions on the principle that a team represents a client more effectively and efficiently than an individual lawyer. Accordingly, although a number of lawyers may work on a particular engagement, we avoid, and will not charge, for redundancy.

*RESPONSES TO AUDITORS' INQUIRIES.* We are frequently asked to provide information to auditing firms regarding legal matters on which we are representing a client. We respond to those inquiries with the same level of care and professionalism that we use to handle the Client's other legal work. Moreover, if an auditing firm requests information on the Client's behalf, that request will be deemed to be the Client's consent for us to disclose that information to that firm.

*DISBURSEMENTS AND CHARGES.* Most matters involve disbursements and charges for various products and services incidental to our legal work, such as document duplicating services, travel, long distance telephone and telecopier services, computerized research (such as LEXIS and Westlaw), courier services, and postage. Some services will be provided by our firm and others by third party vendors. We may advance nominal charges from our Client's account to pay certain vendors. Invoices from other vendors (such as printer, expert witnesses, process servers and court reporters) will be forwarded to the Client directly for payment. We manage our own telephone network, printing and document duplication services. We generally use our in-house printing and document duplicating services rather than third party services, due to timing and confidentiality concerns. We will handle these services however the Client requests. We set our charges for these services based upon our fully burdened cost of providing them to the Client.

*TRAVEL.* We generally record the time spent traveling in furtherance of the Client's engagement at the hourly rates established for the Client matter and take that time into consideration in calculating a fee. Any time spent working on the Client's matters or those of another client while traveling will reduce the amount of any such traveling time considered in calculating the fee and will not be double billed. Air travel is booked at coach rates unless otherwise previously approved by the Client or unless the air travel is transoceanic or overnight, in which case we generally book business or comparable class.

*OVERTIME.* If the Client's work requires our non-exempt personnel to work overtime, we will ask the Client to reimburse us for those expenses. For safety reasons, or lack of readily available alternative means of transportation at night in some of our markets, it may be necessary to use taxi or car hire services rather than normal bus, train, or subway commuting. Such expenses are an appropriate cost of the Client's engagement, and we will pass them along at our direct cost, with no markup.

*STATEMENTS.* We render monthly statements for fees, disbursements, and charges. Separate invoices are normally produced for each legal matter being handled. The Client also will receive a monthly statement which shows any past due invoice, by number and date, for each Client's matters.

*PAYMENT.* Each statement is due upon presentation. Payment is expected within 30 days. Failure to pay statements promptly may result in temporary or permanent cessation of service. Payment of statements should be made in U.S. dollars, by wire transfer or in checks or drafts payable to Jagger Starr & Houston P.C. Please note the date and identification number of the statement being paid, and return the remittance copy of our statement.

*DISENGAGEMENT.* The Client may terminate our engagement by written notice to the Firm. Such termination does not, however, relieve the Client of the obligation to pay for all services rendered and disbursements and other charges paid or incurred on behalf of the Client or in connection with our engagement. We also reserve the right to withdraw from our representation if, for example, the Client fails to honor the terms of the engagement letter, or the Client fails to cooperate or follow our advice on a material matter for any fact or circumstance which would or could, in our view, render our continued representation unlawful or unethical. If we elect to withdraw, the Client will take all steps necessary to free us of any obligation to perform further services, including the execution of any documents necessary to complete our withdrawal, and we will be entitled to be paid for all services rendered and all costs and expenses incurred on behalf of the Client up until the date of the withdrawal.

# ENGAGEMENT LETTER

# (EXAMPLE 2)

Rodriguez Greenberg & Irabu, P.C.
One Unitas Square
1927 Yankee Boulevard
Syracuse, New York 13246

April 17, 2002

Mr. Hylton J. Horning
Chief Executive Officer
Cross–Jupiter Cargo, Inc.
3333 Savannah Road
Albany, New York 12209

Dear Mr. Horning:

We are pleased that Cross–Jupiter Cargo, Inc. ("the Company") has retained us to represent your Company in connection with the Company's contemplated acquisition of Tier Three Cargo Corporation. This letter sets forth the basic terms of our engagement.

We are committed to performing services for you with the utmost loyalty that an attorney owes to his or her client and in accordance with the Rules of Professional Conduct. It may be helpful for us to state the general principles that govern this area. We will, unless you consent otherwise, keep your confidences and avoid any conflict with your interests with respect to this and any other matter in which we are engaged by you. However, as you may know, we represent many other clients in a variety of geographical and subject-matter areas. We therefore undertake this representation and any future representation of you on other matter(s) on the understanding that we are free to represent other client(s) on matters in which you may be adverse or may have an adverse interest, so long as such matters are not substantially related to the work we are doing for you and do not allow for the use of confidential information you have provided to us. If this understanding is not acceptable to you, please notify me immediately. If you want us to consider your corporate parents, subsidiaries, or affiliates in our preclearance process of new matters, please inform me promptly, and please send us (i) a written list of your corporate affiliates; and (ii) a periodic updating of that list.

The lawyer with whom you deal primarily may assign responsibility for completing some of your work to other lawyers or other personnel in this law firm under his or her supervision, and may use other firm lawyers where specialized help is needed. The supervising lawyer will continue to be responsible for your entire assignment, however, and will be available to discuss the use of other personnel with you. It is our goal to assign tasks among lawyers, law clerks, and document clerks in a way that produces the highest quality of work at a reasonable price.

Our fees are ordinarily based on hourly rates for lawyers and various other time chargers such as paraprofessionals. Our rates, of course, reset from time to time, generally at the start of each year. Our current rates for matters such as this range from $220 to $475 for partners, $205 to $350 for "of counsel," $100 to $225 for associates, and $55 to $100 for most categories of paraprofessionals. My current rate is $375, and Ms. Jennifer McGrudy's rate, who will be working on this matter, is $175. We may adjust the charge downward or upward based on other facts such as the novelty or complexity of the issue and problems encountered, the extent of the responsibility involved, the result achieved, the efficiency of our work, the customary fees for similar legal services and other similar factors that will enable us to arrive at a fair fee under the circumstances. Pursuant to our normal practice, our bills also include direct charges for such items as travel expenses, postage, telephone calls, faxes, duplicating, computer network services, computerized research, and secretarial overtime.

In addition, if this engagement requires substantial disbursements by us to third parties, such as consultants, accountants, or other experts, we may request an advance from you of the amounts involved. Otherwise, your financial obligations to us will be reflected in our routine billings.

We will send you monthly statements for our services. (If you have any special policies with respect to information you want in our statements, please advise us promptly so that we can avoid confusion or delay.) Please review our bills when you receive them so that any questions you may have are raised in a timely fashion. We request that our statements be paid within thirty days of receipt, and we reserve the right to discontinue providing legal services, after notice, if our statements are not paid within a reasonable time.

We look forward to working with you on this matter. If you have any questions about any of the arrangements detailed in this letter, please do not hesitate to contact me.

Very truly yours,

______________________________

H. Albert Chiu

## MULTIPLE REPRESENTATION LETTER

Mr. Colin Dupres
1301 Elmhurst Drive
Chicago, IL 60604

Ms. Jennifer Plassius
724 East Juniper Place
Chicago, IL 60611

Re: *Consent to Multiple Representation*

Dear Mr. Dupres and Ms. Plassius:

You have requested that our law firm, Dooley, Chen, McGuire & Goldstein, P.C., represent each of you in the preparation of organizational documents for Dexford Appraisal, LLC.

Our representation of clients is governed by the Illinois Disciplinary Rules of Professional Conduct, as adopted by the Supreme Court of Illinois and State Bar of Illinois.

A lawyer has the duty to exercise independent professional judgment on behalf of each client. When a lawyer is requested to represent multiple clients in the same matter, he can do so if he concludes that he can fulfill this duty with regard to each of the clients on an impartial basis and obtains the consent of each client after an explanation of the possible risks involved in the multiple representation situation. Further, if at any time during the representation it is determined that, because of differences between the joint clients, a lawyer can no longer represent each of the clients impartially, then the lawyer must at that time withdraw from representing all of the clients.

I am hereby advising each of you of your right to obtain separate legal counsel to represent you in all matters. I strongly recommend that course of action to you. I understand that each of you understands this but nevertheless wants our Law Firm to represent both of you in connection with the preparation of the documents referenced above. Based on the information you have provided, we have concluded that we can represent each of you on an impartial basis. In determining whether you should consent to this joint representation, however, you should carefully consider the following matters.

The first matter involves the attorney-client privilege. Although the law is not settled, we believe that any information disclosed by you to us in connection with this representation will not be protected by the privilege in a subsequent legal proceeding asserted by or against one of you involving the other. Moreover, we believe we cannot effectively represent each of you if information disclosed to us by one of you must be preserved by us in confidence from the other. If we are to represent you, it will only be with the express understanding that each of you has waived the attorney-client privilege to the extent, but only to the extent, that the privilege might otherwise require us to preserve in confidence information disclosed by one of you to us from the other.

An additional point is that, if either of you divulges information to anyone except the other one or members of my firm, the privilege would probably be waived, at least in part. The extent of that loss is not clear. It might relate only to the actual content of the specific communication. It could, however, involve related information.

Second, at this time there does not appear to be any difference of opinion between you with regard to the terms of the LLC member agreement or any of the other documents. However, it may turn out, upon further consultation, that one or more of you may have varying opinions with respect to the tax classification of the entity, valuation of contributed assets, allocations of profits and losses, sharing of expenses, distributions, buy-out provisions, management or other matters. It is our duty to explore each of these issues with you. Should we determine that there are material differences between you on one or more of these issues that you cannot resolve on an amicable basis or that we conclude cannot be resolved on terms compatible with the best interests of each party involved, then we must at that time withdraw from the representation. If this occurs, we will, if you wish, assist each of you in obtaining new counsel. If we must withdraw, there may be an added expense caused by the representation by a new law firm.

We understand that each of you will be responsible for payment of our legal fees, filing fees and any other out-of-pocket expenses.

As is true with all legal services, we cannot and do not guarantee the results of our representation. We cannot and do not make any warranties express or implied with regard to our representation.

If you are willing to consent to our joint representation based on the disclosures and conditions listed above, please so indicate in the spaces provided below and return one copy of this letter to us.

Very truly yours,

____________________

Alexandra Frankel for
Dooley, Chen, McGuire &
Goldman, P.C.

We consent to your joint representation of us on the conditions set forth in this letter.

Date: ________________ ____________________
Colin Dupres

Date: ________________ ____________________
Jennifer Plassius

## MULTIPLE REPRESENTATION PROVISION

As you know, this Firm will be representing other clients in this Matter in addition to yourself. The co-clients are Lucky Beverage, Inc. and Mr. Cecil Hazeltine. Although your interests and those of the co-clients currently appear to coincide, there is a potential conflict of interest in every multiple representation. For example, you or the co-clients or one or more of them may subsequently decide to pursue different and inconsistent courses of action if circumstances change or for some other reason. You understand that if such a conflict arises the Firm may be forced to withdraw from representing one or more of its clients and that, as a result, you could incur additional expenses and inconvenience in securing substitute counsel.

The confidentiality of your communications to the Firm cannot be as secure in the case of multiple representation as they would be if you were separately represented. Secrets or confidences that you share with this Firm may be disclosed to the co-clients, and the privilege that ordinarily shields attorney-client communications from disclosure to third parties could be lost in the future if a co-client becomes adverse to you and discloses such communications to third parties. Of course, as in every representation, the Firm will in every other respect maintain the confidentiality of all privileged or proprietary materials provided to us by you in the course of our representation.

By your signature below you confirm your agreement to the terms of this multiple representation and your waiver of any actual or potential conflicts that may exist as a result of the Firm's joint representation of you and the Firm's co-clients in this matter.

____________________________

Jessica J. Bandera

Dated: July 17, 2002

## WAIVER OF CONFLICT LETTER

MANTEL BONDS & THOMPSON, P.C.
300 Triple Way
Brooklyn, NY 11201

May 30, 2002

Board of Directors
Sosa Foods Corporation
230 Slugger Avenue
Brooklyn, NY 11201

Re: *Waiver of Conflict–Sosa Foods Corporation*

Dear Board Members:

As you know, Mantel Bonds & Thompson, P.C. (the "Firm") has served as counsel to Sosa Foods Corporation (the "Company") and has represented the Company with respect to various matters, including the Company's efforts to obtain financing. The Company has reiterated its request that the Firm assist the Company with respect to those efforts.

The Firm has identified a potential source of financing for the Company (the "Investment Opportunity"). However, that financing would be derived from an existing and longstanding client of the Firm and/or associated entities of that client (hereafter, the "Maris Entities"). The purpose of this letter is to confirm that you are aware of this representation and that you waive any such conflict. In order for us to assist in this potential financing, it is necessary that both the Company and the Maris Entities: (i) acknowledge their awareness of this Firm's conflict of interest stemming from our prior representation of both potential parties to the Investment Opportunity; and (ii) waive the conflict of interest that exists, with the understanding that this Firm will then represent the Maris Entities in connection with the Investment Opportunity and not the Company.

We do not believe that our prior representation of the Company or of the Maris Entities will adversely affect our professional responsibility owed to the Company or to the Maris Entities with respect to the Investment Opportunity.

However, you must be aware that through its representation of the Company the Firm has become aware of certain non-public information adverse to the Company and individual members of the Board which would be disclosed to the Maris Entities. By signing this waiver letter you expressly recognize that such adverse information would be disclosed and consent to that disclosure.

The Company should and must retain separate counsel to represent it with respect to the Investment Opportunity. As required by the Rules of Professional Responsibility, the Firm will not represent the Maris Entities and will not assist in the Investment Opportunity absent a waiver by the Company and separate counsel being retained by the Company.

By execution of this letter in the space provided below, we are requesting that you waive any existing conflict of interest with respect to the Investment Opportunity as outlined above.

Please indicate your acknowledgment and consent by signing a copy of this letter in the space provided below and returning it to us.

Very truly yours,

MANTEL BONDS AND THOMPSON, P.C.

By:________________

Homer Roth

AGREED TO AND ACCEPTED:

SOSA FOODS
CORPORATION

By:__________________
C. Striker Clemens

## TERMINATION OF ENGAGEMENT PROVISION

This engagement will terminate at the end of the matter described in this letter. In any event, unless we agree otherwise in writing, this engagement will be deemed terminated if the matter has been inactive and the Firm has had no occasion to perform any legal services in connection with it for a period of one year. You will have the right to terminate this engagement at any time and for any reason. The Firm also reserves the right to do so if our statements are not timely paid, or for any other reason required or permitted by the applicable rules of professional conduct.

# JOINT DEFENSE AGREEMENT

This Joint Defense Agreement is entered into by and among the Parties and by and among counsel for Kilarney Industries Corp. and counsel for Mack McLiew and Sylvia Abbott on or about this 16 day of July 2002. Kilarney Industries Corp., Mack McLiew and Sylvia Abbott are referred to herein as the "Parties."

WHEREAS, the undersigned are aware of the proceeding being conducted by the U.S. Department of Justice (DOJ), and the respective clients of the undersigned have been requested to provide information to the DOJ or expect that they may be requested or compelled to provide information to the DOJ; and

WHEREAS, the undersigned believe that it is in the mutual interest of their clients to pursue a joint defense in connection with this proceeding; and

NOW, THEREFORE, IT IS AGREED as follows:

1. The Parties agree to pursue a joint defense effort, for the sole purpose of facilitating their joint defense of such claims or charges as may be made against them, their officers, agents or affiliates in connection with or arising out of the above-referenced DOJ proceeding.

2. The Parties agree that members of the joint defense team will share information for the sole purpose of furthering such joint defense, and that all information so exchanged will be kept confidential and will not be revealed to persons outside the joint defense team. The confidential pooling of information among members of the joint defense team is not intended to waive any attorney-client privilege or work product privilege that may be applicable to such material.

3. The joint defense team includes:

(a) The Parties;

(b) Their attorneys, including Dustin J. Gray of the law firm of Hansen, Avila, Hu & Tresh, PC—counsel for Kilarney Industries Corp; Suzanne A.

Torres of McKinney Swarz, RLLP—counsel for Mack McLiew; and Joseph J. Lazzano of Harrison Knoor & Sweeney, LLC—counsel for Sylvia Abbott; co-counsel who are associated with the same law firms as any of the aforementioned attorneys and who assist in the joint defense effort, and any in-house counsel of the respective Parties who assist in the joint defense effort.

4. The Parties agree that all information shared pursuant to this agreement shall be used solely in connection with the above-referenced DOJ proceeding and any related proceedings resulting from it.

In order to memorialize this ongoing joint defense effort, the Parties, through their authorized attorneys, execute this Agreement on the dates set opposite their respective names.

Date: July 16, 2002 By: ______________________
DUSTIN J. GRAY

Date: July 16, 2002 By: ______________________
SUZANNE A. TORRES

Dated: July 16, 2002 By: ______________________
JOSEPH J. LAZZANO

## "TIPS" TO AVOID MALPRACTICE

*(1) Client "In–Take" Procedures*—It is surprising how little due diligence many law firms undertake when determining whether to accept a new client. Frequently, only a conflicts check is conducted with little or no scrutiny by firm lawyers regarding the prospective client's background. Some lawyers view their job as "fixing the client's dilemma" as soon as practicable. Unfortunately, the scenario too often arises that the client's dilemma becomes the lawyer's problem. Clients with previous regulatory problems, bankruptcy history, and fraud actions fall into this category. Steps that should be taken to minimize the in-take of unsavory clients include, for example, after receiving prospective client consent, making thorough inquiry of predecessor counsel, having discussions with the client's accountant and predecessor accountants (if feasible), conducting searches on LEXIS–NEXIS and WestLaw, and making appropriate client references with third parties.

*(2) Written Letter of Engagement*—Before accepting a client, an attorney should insist on the execution of a letter of engagement setting forth the essentials of the representation. A letter of engagement should contain, for example, the identity of the client(s), the scope of the engagement, the amount of any retainer required, the fees to be charged by the attorneys, paralegals, and other personnel working on the matter(s), the costs (such as duplicating, courier fees, and court costs) to be incurred by the client(s), the terms upon which counsel may withdraw from the representation, and multiple representation disclosures (and client consents) that are applicable.

By executing a letter of engagement that clearly sets forth and limits the scope of the engagement, malpractice liability exposure may be minimized. For example, a number of courts hold that, in connection with drafting a client's offering documents, counsel owes the client a duty to conduct due diligence (including the making of independent inquiry) with respect to the accuracy and sufficiency of the disclosures made.[1] If the scope of the engagement has been limited so that counsel does not undertake this task (and such is clearly stated in the engagement letter), attorney liability normally should be averted. Of course, if significant "red flags" come to counsel's attention, limitations on the scope of engagement may not provide shelter for the subject attorney.[2]

*(3) Written Letters to the Client and/or Memos to the File*—Frequently, counsel renders oral legal advice to a client, declining to provide any written back-up to the advice proffered. When the client does not follow that advice and problems surface based on the issues covered by such advice, the danger exists that the client will assert that no such advice in fact was ever given. Without any written documentation to support that such advice indeed was provided, the affected client's suit for malpractice may withstand motions for summary judgment, thereby leaving the issue to the factfinder (namely, the jury) to determine who is telling the truth. In such event, settlement may be the most viable alternative.

To avoid this catastrophe, counsel would be prudent to write the client confirming the oral advice rendered. Indeed, when the significance of the oral advice is clear, counsel customarily should follow-up in writing. Often, however, only with the benefit of hindsight does the importance of the oral advice emerge. Moreover, writing of continuous letters to clients may well be time-consuming, incur seemingly unnecessary legal fees, and impair client relations. To accommodate these concerns, when an attorney orally counsels a client on an apparently significant issue, writing a "Memo to the File" to

**1.** *See, e.g., FDIC v. O'Melveny & Myers*, 969 F.2d 744 (9th Cir.1992), *rev'd on other grounds*, 512 U.S. 79 (1994).

**2.** *See generally* Donohue, *Attorney Liability in the Preparation of Securities Disclosures Documents—Limiting Liability in the Face of Expanded Duties*, 18 Sec. Reg. L. J. 115 (1990); Warren, *The Primary Liability of Securities Lawyers*, 50 SMU L. Rev. 383 (1996).

document electronically and time date the oral advice given would be prudent. This "solution" is practical, takes at most five to ten minutes, and maintains good client relations. If consistently and adequately implemented, this practice lessens the risk of attorney malpractice exposure.

*(4) Termination and "Change of Scope" Letters*—When a law firm completes the matter(s) with respect to which it was retained, a letter of termination should be sent to the client setting forth such termination. A termination letter is helpful in at least two important ways. First, it eliminates the argument that the subject party reasonably believed that the law firm was still engaged in the representation, being responsible to address pertinent legal dilemmas. Second, a termination letter greatly aids in distinguishing present from former clients for attorney conflict of interest purposes. Undoubtedly, the conflict rules are far more stringent with respect to current clients. An effectively written termination letter significantly reduces a law firm's exposure to successful disqualification motions as well as malpractice actions.

A practice that evidently is not customarily implemented today is to write an existing client a letter communicating that the scope of representation has changed. Such a letter should effectively diffuse a client's assertion that, although the firm had not billed the client with respect to the alleged deficient matter(s), the client, as a current client looking to the scope of representation as set forth in the engagement letter, reasonably believed that the law firm continued to be its counsel with respect to such matter(s).[3]

An example illustrates this situation. At the inception of the representation, the engagement letter provides that the law firm Doolittle & Cartright, P.C. represents Jana Tarzana, Inc. with respect to general

**3.** *See In re Rexplore Inc. Securities Litigation*, 685 F.Supp. 1132 (N.D.Cal.1988).

corporate work, securities offerings and SEC filings, transactional matters, and trademark infringement litigation. At that time, Doolittle & Cartright is the only law firm representing Jana Tarzana in corporate/securities matters, thereby clearly serving as the outside general counsel with respect to those matters. Ten months later, Jana Tarzana elects to hire three additional law firms to service its corporate/securities work. Indeed, within two years of its original retention as counsel to Jana Tarzana, Doolittle & Cartright's representation is limited to sporadic transactional work and two relatively small litigation matters. Subsequently, due to misappropriation perpetrated by its insiders, Jana Tarzana becomes insolvent. Plaintiff's counsel on behalf of aggrieved shareholders initiates suit in state court against Doolittle & Cartright alleging that as general outside counsel to Jana Tarzana the law firm was negligent in its oversight role and substantially assisted the fraud through its reckless disregard. These allegations may survive motions to dismiss and for summary judgment, thereby becoming issues for the jury.

An appropriately phrased letter to the Client (here Jana Tarzana, Inc.) setting forth changes in the scope of the engagement would have greatly diminished the risk that the subject law firm could have reasonably been viewed by the client as maintaining its position as general outside counsel. In addition to lessening liability exposure for the law firm, client misunderstanding on this subject would be avoided. The client will be informed that, if it so elects, it must have another law firm to act as outside general counsel or, alternatively, must reinvigorate the relationship with the subject law firm. Given the stakes implicated, prudent counsel today should endeavor to write such "change of scope" letters to affected clients.

*(5) Multiple Representation—Client Waiver*

Potential conflicts of interest arising from multiple representation arise with regularity. Such potential conflict dilemmas occur in both the transactional and litigation settings. A common perception held by attorneys is that conflicts may be waived by the affected clients with their informed consent after such clients are provided with adequate disclosure of the applicable circumstances and consequences of such joint representation. However, although such informed client consent is a necessary prerequisite, it alone is not sufficient. In addition, even if informed client consent is procured, in order to undertake (or continue with) the multiple representation, a disinterested lawyer should reasonably believe that such representation will not materially adversely affect each of the client's best interests.[4] This latter condition adds great uncertainty to the propriety of proceeding with multiple representation in troublesome situations, irrespective of client consent. Particularly (but not solely) when the clients are relatively unsophisticated, the attorney should be wary of undertaking joint representation. Examples where prudent counsel normally should avoid multiple representation include representing the buyer and seller in the sale of a business; the corporation and its publicly-held subsidiary in a related party transaction; and the corporation and its directors in a derivative action involving serious allegations of insider wrongdoing.[5] In such situations, separate counsel normally should be retained.

*(6) Supervision of Associates*

Although obvious in theory, lapses that too often occur relate to inadequate supervision of recent law school graduates. Perhaps due to (1) the entry of dozens of new associates each year in major law firms, (2) the time and client pressures placed on more senior attorneys, and (3) the mammoth size of many firms, thereby sometimes culminating in the inefficient allocation of oversight resources, the risk exists that inexperienced associates will be unduly left on their own to perpetrate malpractice. Fortunately, as a general proposition, law firms are astutely addressing these concerns in an effec-

**4.** *See* ABA Model Rule 1.7 & cmt. 15.

**5.** *See Messing v. FDI*, Inc., 439 F.Supp. 776 (D.N.J.1977).

tive manner to diminish their liability exposure, properly train their associates, and aptly serve their clients.

*(7) Senior Partner Oversight Dilemmas*

Unlike the associate supervision issue, numerous law firms ignore or neglect an equally important dilemma: that a senior partner who has leverage in the firm monopolizes "his" (or "her") client over a period of time, loses the requisite degree of objectivity, and becomes co-opted (with the firm) in the client's misconduct. Unfortunately, this scenario occurs with some frequency. The reasons why there is a dearth of co-partner oversight are relatively straightforward: the senior partner has a stable of premier clients generating handsome revenues and prestige for the law firm; other senior lawyers with clients of their "own" have affinity and respect for the subject partner; these lawyers trust that the subject partner will provide capable representation; and lower-tier attorneys in the firm fear reprisal if they become too active in questioning the advice rendered by the senior partner. To alleviate this situation, each law firm should assess its own culture to develop a suitable response. It is clear, however, that an increasing number of attorney liability cases invoke the senior partner lack of objectivity dilemma.

*(8) Investing in Clients*

Being an investor in a client or taking fees in stock increases the threat of liability. The anticipation of lucrative economic returns may justify this risk.[6] However, the presence of such an economic stake enables plaintiffs' lawyers to posture before the jury the motivations underlying counsel's alleged misconduct in concealing or aiding the client's fraud. Simply put, without the consummation of the offering involving materially misleading disclosure documents, the attorneys' remuneration would have been greatly diminished. Jurors earning $20,000 annually will listen intently when in-

**6.** See American Bar Association, *Acquiring Ownership In A Client In Connection with Performing Legal Services*, Formal Opinion No. 00–418 (2000).

formed that a successful public offering resulted in the defendant law firm's receipt of stock then valued at $1 million. Law firms electing to invest in clients or take their fees in stock should be cognizant of their enhanced liability exposure.

*(9) Counsel Serving as Director*

For the lawyer in a small firm seeking to procure publicly-held corporations as clients, acting as an "outside" director may be a justifiable economic risk. Of course, a lawyer should do so only if adequate director and officer liability and attorney malpractice insurance is procured. For attorneys with more established practices, serving in the dual role of counsel and director makes little sense. Case law makes clear that the attorney/director is subject to enhanced standards. Concerns relating to privilege preservation and insurance coverage arise with some frequency. Accordingly, prudent counsel should attend board of director and appropriate committee meetings serving only as counsel.[7]

*Conclusion*

In conclusion, corporate/securities counsel today often labors in a "minefield" where scrupulous adherence to ethical standards and the conducting of "self" due diligence are key components of avoiding liability. The "tips" provided in this Appendix are not guarantees. But effective implementation of the suggestions proffered should go a long way to decrease the risk of liability.

**7.** *See Escott v. BarChris Construction Corp.*, 283 F.Supp. 643 (S.D.N.Y.1968); Block, Meierholfer & Wallach, *Lawyers Serving on the Boards of Directors of Clients: A Survey of the Problems*, 7 Insights No. 4, at 3 (April 1993); "Lawyer–Directors Are Key Targets for Plaintiffs' Lawyers, ABA Group Told," 21 Sec. Reg. & L. Rep. (BNA) 1272 (1989) (asserting that attorneys who serve as directors of their clients "have to be 'certifiably nuts' "); Williams, *The Role of Inside Counsel in Corporate Accountability*, [1979–1980 Transfer Binder] CCH Fed. Sec. L. Rep. ¶ 82,318, at 82,375 (1979) (presented as then SEC Chairman).

†